Dedicated to all the amazing storytellers I have met and learnt from on my journey so far, and to those I am yet to meet and be inspired by in the future.

About the author

With a career in advertising and marketing spanning nearly thirty years, James has worked in all areas of marketing from media to brand strategy and was also a pioneer of digital advertising from its earliest days.

During his career, he has also founded three highly successful agencies.

The first Media Business North is now part of the global media agency network Mediacom.

The second Diffiniti, became the most prominent digital media agency in the U.K. and later evolved into the iProspect network.

In more recent years, he has been Chief Digital Officer for U.M. and IPG Media brands and the head of International Agency Relationships for AOL, as well as Chief Digital & Data Officer for the global media agency Carat while most recently, he was the Global Chief Strategy Officer for Mindshare before moving to his current WPP Global Planning role.

Renowned for his storytelling experience and expertise, when not using this to advance the world of advertising, he is also a skilled practitioner of the ancient arts of both origami and Kung Fu (in which he holds a black belt).

In recent years James has also been a vocal and passionate campaigner for Neuro Divergence following his diagnosis with ADHD & ASD in later life, describing it as the superpower behind his successful career.

"Storytelling, as it turns out, was crucial to our evolution, more so than opposable thumbs.

Opposable thumbs let us hang on; stories told us what to hang on to."

Lisa Cron Author of Wired for Story

Contents

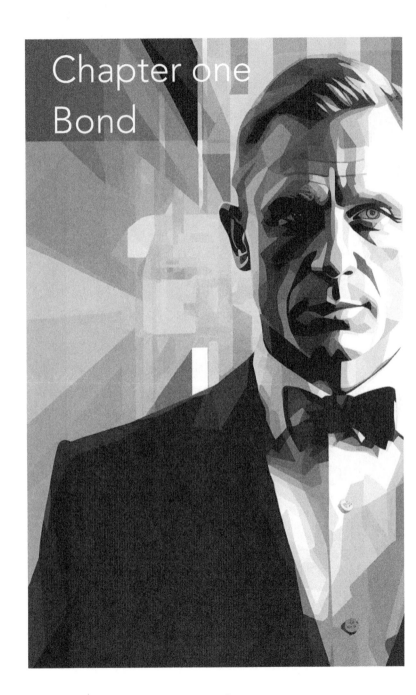

Chapter one
Bond

Scan to begin.

So, who doesn't, even if they may not openly admit it, enjoy a James Bond movie?

Yes, some older movies may no longer fit our modern and much better standards for appropriate behaviours and gender portrayal whilst at the same time, some special effects may now appear dated and naive compared to modern CGI.

But the simple reality is that James Bond has been around as a storytelling franchise for over 60 years.

And what is more, as evidenced by the short movie you have hopefully just watched in celebration of that fact, it looks set to excite and entertain audiences for many more.

So, indulge me momentarily, and let us explore some further Bond-inspired imagination.

Picture this: it's the twilight of 2021 or perhaps the dawn of 2022.

You've just enjoyed viewing the latest James Bond movie, "No Time to Die".

You're still under the enchanting spell of this cinematic masterpiece, which has more than done justice to the legendary Bond franchise.

The plot, the performances, the cinematography - everything was top-notch and kept you on the edge of your seat.

Yet, as the credits rolled and you left the theatre, you were comfortably aware it was all just an illusion.

This brilliantly crafted fictional tale doesn't have the power to cross the boundary into reality or significantly influence your future actions.

Or does it?

Please permit me to share an intriguing observation with you.

As you strolled away from the cinema, still basking in the afterglow of the thrilling film, you happened to cross paths with a high-end watch store.

In its beautifully illuminated window was displayed the same Omega speed master watch that Daniel Craig, the man himself, wore with unmatched elegance in the movie.

It even flaunted the unique, limited edition 007 branding.

Involuntarily, you found your footsteps halting and your eyes riveted to the exquisitely crafted timepiece showcased behind the glass.

Captivated by its allure, a curious thought emerges from your mind, "What if?"

This powerful question held you in its grip, urging you to explore the possibilities.

Unable to resist the pull of curiosity, you push open the door and enter the store.

You request that the assistant allow you to experience the watch first hand, to feel the cold, smooth metal against your skin and see the polished dial on your wrist.

Suddenly, you are longer just imagining.

As the Omega Speed master snuggly fits around your wrist, you feel an intoxicating wave of transformation – a sensation of stepping into Bond's shoes.

Without further ado, you decided to make the timepiece yours, undeterred by its steep price.

For a fleeting moment, you even entertained the thought of stopping at the Aston Martin dealership on your journey home, but common sense and financial reality make that no more than a fleeting thought.

But how could this be?

How did a fictional world manage to seep into your real-life decisions?

Welcome to the magical universe of storytelling.

As this real scenario suggests, storytelling isn't just about weaving tales.

It can alter our perceptions, stir our emotions, and shape our actions in ways we often don't realize.

This transformation is achieved through two mechanisms.

Firstly, storytelling bestows upon an object the power of provenance.

The dictionary defines provenance as 'A record of ownership of a work of art or an antique, used as a guide to authenticity or quality.' In simpler terms, the backstory breathes life into an otherwise lifeless object.

For instance, take the auction of an Aston Martin DB5, an event that transpired in 2019.

The occasion was a high-profile auction but not your average affair with priceless art or rare antiques.

Instead, it was an auction that held centre-stage, an embodiment of cinematic history and automotive finesse – The 007 Aston Martin DB5.

This chariot of speed and elegance graced the silver screen alongside the quintessential embodiment of sophistication and courage - none other than James Bond himself.

The car wasn't merely a vehicle; it was a co-star, sharing screen time, adventures, and the aura of danger and glamour that encapsulates the Bond franchise in several memorable films.

At this point, one might ponder the price tag of such an esteemed piece of cinematic history and mechanical craftsmanship.

Given its connection to Bond, it's a given that the car would command a price higher than usual.

But just how much more would a buyer be willing to shell out?

Would it be near half a million dollars, which is already a sizable sum?

Or could it reach the million-dollar mark, a testament to the car's unique history?

Could it be even higher, venturing into the territory of two million dollars?

Prepare to be astounded because the actual sum is far beyond these estimates.

This Aston Martin DB5, an embodiment of cinematic history, nostalgia, and sheer luxury, was sold for an astronomical $6.4 million!

To put this into perspective, it's worth noting that the DB5 is indeed a classic beauty.

Even without its James Bond connection, it's a car that represents the pinnacle of British automotive luxury and design.

As a vintage vehicle, it is highly sought after by car enthusiasts and collectors worldwide, with such vehicles typically being valued around the half-million-dollar mark.

But the astonishing $6.4 million price tag for this DB5 goes far beyond its mechanical merits.

It reflects the car's iconic status and association with one of cinema's most enduring characters.

It underscores the power of narrative, history, and cultural resonance in adding value to an object - turning a classic car into a piece of cherished cinematic legacy.

The extraordinary price it commanded was due to its provenance – the captivating narrative woven around it through its appearances in the James Bond film franchise.

And what is more, this captivating principle, the intriguing notion that an object's origin and accompanying narrative can drastically alter its perceived worth, isn't confined to luxury items or high-end collectables.

It is a universal truth, a phenomenon that transcends boundaries, categories, and price tags, it is far-reaching and inclusive, affecting objects from various backgrounds, not just those with opulence or rarity.

This principle has its roots deeply embedded in the fabric of our lives, permeating not only our material possessions but also our personal experiences, traditions, and cultural practices.

From a child's cherished teddy bear to a family heirloom passed down through generations, from a simple handmade craft to an item of sentimental value gifted by a loved one, the backstory, the narrative of origin, the emotional connection, and the memories associated with these objects amplify their value to us beyond any price tag.

Whether it's the clay pot you shaped with your hands in an art class, the pebble you picked up on a memorable beach vacation, or even the humble book passed down in your family, each holds a value far more significant than its intrinsic or market value.

The stories they tell, the memories they evoke, and the emotions they stir make them priceless.

This is a testament to the power and influence of storytelling, a universal human experience that shapes our perception of value and meaning.

So, when we say that this fascinating principle of origin is not just limited to luxury items, we acknowledge its wide-ranging impact, ability to touch every facet of our lives, and remarkable power to turn the ordinary into something precious.

The implications of this principle are vast and transformative, encouraging us to look beyond the surface, appreciate the hidden narratives of the world around us, and recognize that value often resides in the stories that objects tell rather than the objects themselves.

It is a universally acknowledged truth that irrespective of its intrinsic monetary value, any object has the potential to harness the power of a gripping narrative to amplify its perceived worth substantially.

An object's worth does not always lie solely in its physical material or craftsmanship. Sometimes, it's the story that surrounds it that truly sets its value.

This idea has been intriguingly demonstrated in the Significant Objects Project, an ingenious experiment curated by Rob Walker and Joshua Glenn.

This inventive project, found at www.significantobjects.com, was more than just an exercise in creativity.

It was a tangible endeavour that aimed to demonstrate, with concrete evidence, that the influence of a well-crafted narrative on an object's value could be objectively measured and quantified.

At the heart of this experiment lay two hundred mundane, seemingly inconsequential thrift-store trinkets. These were not rare artefacts or prized collector's items but ordinary everyday items one might overlook without a second glance.

However, they were about to become the stars of a grand experiment that would challenge and redefine traditional notions of value.

Each of these trinkets, regardless of their inherent worth, was put up for auction on the popular online marketplace eBay.

But these auctions were no ordinary listings. Alongside each trinket was a unique short story meticulously crafted by one of over two hundred contributing writers.

Each narrative brought the seemingly insignificant item to life, transforming it from a simple trinket into a protagonist of its tale.

These items' initial average purchase price was a modest $1.25, reflecting their perceived insignificance, but when their auctions ended, the results were nothing short of astonishing.

The two hundred trinkets, given value by their respective narratives, raised nearly $8,000!

The significance of this outcome is profound.

It not only underlines but boldly highlights in indelible ink the incredible power of storytelling to enhance the value of an object.

It offers irrefutable evidence that even an object of low inherent worth can be transformed through the simple yet powerful tool of a captivating narrative.

This project shows us that value is not always intrinsic; often, it's the story that we attach to an object that genuinely determines its worth.

The concept of provenance is part of storytelling's broader, more profound impact: its unparalleled ability to supersede our rational thoughts and actions with those that may appear irrational.

This is the seductive power of exceptional storytelling – it's the 'sex, drugs, and rock n roll' of narratives and primarily the hypnotic allure of the 'drugs' aspect, because a well-crafted story can physiologically alter your brain chemistry, influencing your emotional responses and behaviours.

What's even more mind-boggling is that you cannot resist this chemical transformation!

Of course, you might readily accept this concept when applied to the context of highly impactful films where the idea that a narrative can add value is far from alien when we think about the cinematic experience.

Indeed, we often associate movies with profound stories that move us, evoke emotions, and leave lasting impressions, enhancing the value of the film in our eyes.

However, what if I propose that the same principle, this concept of the transformative power of narratives, applies equally to a medium that might seem quite distant from the world of art and storytelling - advertisements?

Yes, you heard it right, advertisements - those short promotional videos or images we encounter daily, interspersed between our favourite television shows, popping up on our social media feeds, or crowding the billboards along highways.

Upon hearing this proposition, you may be sceptical.

An eyebrow might lift in incredulous surprise, questioning how the seemingly mundane world of advertisements could hold a candle to the potent narratives of film.

Advertisements, after all, are often seen as simple, straightforward tools aimed at promoting a product or service, not something that could stir emotions or add value through a compelling narrative.

But let's not dwell on theoretical discussions or abstract debates.

Words, while powerful, can sometimes fall short when trying to illustrate a concept that may seem a little out of the ordinary.

So instead of waxing eloquently on this idea, allow me to provide tangible proof and substantiate this intriguing claim with a straightforward yet compelling experiment.

Prepare yourself for an interactive journey in which we'll delve into the captivating world of advertisements and their narratives.

In the upcoming chapter, we will explore first-hand the narrative power of ads, even the most concise ones and experience how these short promotional materials weave engaging stories, stir emotions, and enhance the perceived value of the products or services they promote.

Chapter two
Science

The universe is made of stories, not of atoms.

Muriel Rukeyser - poet

As I share with you the science of storytelling, I will take you through the narratives of three distinct commercials, and I invite you to witness these stories first hand by scanning a Q.R. code with your mobile device.

These stories won't merely entertain or inform you; they're specially designed to evoke a chemical reaction in your brain.

You might even say they're intended to 'drug' you.

Yes, you heard that right. Drug you.

The goal here is to administer a form of 'cognitive doping.'

But this isn't as ominous as it might seem before you panic.

It's an entirely natural phenomenon that we will tap into for a purpose, and I assure you that unless you're not of this earth, there's no way you can resist this powerful human biochemistry.

So, if you're still up for an exciting intellectual adventure, let's begin our first story, ' THE LAUNCH.'

If you have your mobile device to hand, I urge you to scan the Q.R. code on the next page to watch this gripping tale, but if that's not feasible for you, I will also provide a descriptive narrative to set the scene.

'THE LAUNCH'

Scan to watch.

Our story commences at a spacecraft launch pad, with an impressive shuttle poised for lift-off.

The camera pans out slowly, capturing the tense atmosphere, as we hear a voice echoing in the background, "Mars mission, give me a go, no go for launch..."

This is quickly followed by gripping scenes of technicians scurrying around, undertaking last-minute preparations.

The scene then shifts to a young, wide-eyed child brimming with excitement and anticipation. As the boy watches, the countdown begins, "10," "9," "8," "7"...

However, the thrilling progress is abruptly interrupted by a phone call.

A frantic voice exclaims, "It's the sponsor. Data shows that we need to make the logo bigger," leaving everyone uncertain.

We then cut back to the launch pad, where the spacecraft is now embellished with a massive Astro Boost energy drink logo, dramatically altering the image we associate with a space shuttle.

As the scene unfolds, the countdown resumes, "10," "9," "8," "7"... only to be halted once again by another intrusive phone call.

This time, the news is even more bizarre. "It's the sponsors again. Data shows that millennials don't like the colour," the caller announces, adding, "And we need a hashtag."

Returning to the launch pad, we find the rocket has undergone another extreme makeover. The space vehicle is now smeared in garish shades of orange and green, sporting a colossal hashtag—#MARS—on either side of the boosters.

As the countdown kicks off yet again, another unexpected phone call interrupts the launch.

This time, the sponsors have an even more outrageous demand. "Search data shows Mars is no longer trending. They want to send them to Pluto."

"Pluto?" A baffled launch controller exclaims. Cut to the astronauts within the spacecraft; their confusion is mirrored as one cries out, "Pluto? It's not even a planet!"

Regardless, the countdown resumes once more, and this time it carries on unhindered, "10," "9," "8," "7", "6," "5," "4," "3," "2"...

But just as the countdown approaches the final number, a power cut brings everything to a grinding halt.

"What happened?" A confused voice echoes, only to be answered with a disheartening, "Sorry guys, they burnt up their budget. We have to push the launch to Q4."

The room fills with disgruntlement and frustration, and it's revealed that this was all part of an Adobe marketing product commercial.

So with this tale, I've hopefully triggered a dopamine rush in your brain.

Dopamine, a naturally occurring neurochemical, is often associated with the addictive power of social media and its FOMO (fear of missing out) model. However, dopamine plays an even more significant role in our physiology—it aids in improving focus and concentration. It also enhances memory and motivation.

Reflect on the narrative of the launch.

Weren't you engrossed in it, wondering what would happen next?

Didn't the story motivate you to remember the events as they unfolded and heighten your desire to follow the plot to its conclusion? This kind of audience engagement is incredibly beneficial for storytellers and presenters.

How do you achieve this, you might wonder?

The answer is creating anticipation, suspense, and curiosity, as the launch story successfully does.

Curiosity about what's happening, what comes next, and the reason behind certain decisions all work in tandem to generate dopamine in your brain, enhancing the overall experience of the story.

However, this is just one aspect of the neuroscience of storytelling.

Let's move on to our second commercial, 'THE READER,' introducing you to a new element of this fascinating science, which I will reveal at the end.

Again, you can follow this story by scanning the Q.R. code below with your mobile device. but if that's not possible, I'll once again provide you with a comprehensive account in words.

'THE READER'

Scan to watch.

The story begins with an elderly man in a bookshop, purchasing an instructional book entitled 'Reading Matters.'

As he leaves the store, he glances at the window display which features a newly released, but seemingly random book.

In the following scenes, the man attends an adult literacy class, learning and practising the alphabet.

He's also seen playing Scrabble in a pub, where he humorously misspells the word 'cat' and gets scolded by his friends.

Through a montage of scenes, we see his progress from basic books to more complex ones, and he finally masters spelling 'cat' in Scrabble.

With time, the man continues to read increasingly intricate books.

His hard work culminates with applause and a gold star from his literacy class.

We see him proudly reading the new book he had eyed in the bookshop window.

The final scene unfolds with him approaching the book's author, who recognizes him as his father.

The old man tells the author, "Son, I read your book," leaving the author speechless and the audience even more so, when the narrative concludes with the unexpected revelation that this poignant tale was a commercial for whiskey, not adult literacy.

So, by now, the heart-warming narrative of 'THE READER' likely filled your system with oxytocin—often known as the 'human drug.'

Oxytocin fosters empathy, trust, generosity, and bonding.

As you followed the older man's journey to literacy, you probably felt a connection with him, experienced his triumphs and setbacks, and celebrated his ultimate victory.

And finally, our chemical storytelling journey continues with another element I will administer through our third and final narrative.

We've explored some intriguing narratives thus far, each one designed to stimulate a unique response within you.

We've seen how the power of storytelling can engender a rush of dopamine, fostering focus and concentration, or a surge of oxytocin, promoting empathy and connection.

Now, I wish to share with you a story that is, unapologetically, my all-time favourite.

It is a tale that will tickle your funny bone, releasing a third chemical I shall reveal at the end, so allow me to guide you through our third and final commercial, an unforgettable spectacle titled 'ASTRONAUT.'

Yet again, you are welcome to experience the story first hand by scanning the Q.R. code leading you to the commercial, but if circumstances prevent you from doing so, fret not as I'll ensure you can still appreciate this hilarious and engaging narrative by sharing it as best I can in words.

'ASTRONAUT'

Scan to watch.

Our tale unfolds in the stark, uninviting landscape of space where a group of astronauts, clad in bulky space suits, gather around a vast, gaping crater— a sight to behold against the backdrop of a desolate moonscape.

Then, a creature of unparalleled ugliness erupts from within the crater—a space monster.

In addition to its menacing appearance, this monstrous entity appears to suffer from acute anger management issues.

With a fearsome scowl and a swipe of its formidable claws, the space monster sends the first astronaut flying.

The second and third astronauts fare no better, each being swiftly dispatched by the enraged creature and slammed with immense force into the moon's powdery surface.

Yet, there remains one astronaut who escapes the space monster's wrath.

Concealed behind a large rock, this final astronaut manages to evade the creature's rampage.

His heart pounds in his chest as he watches the monster relentlessly scour the area in search of him.

What feels like an eternity passes.

The monstrous entity, unable to find the last astronaut, concedes defeat.

It turns around and begins to lumber away, leaving the astronaut breathless but alive.

The crisis, it seems, has now passed.

But in this silent moonscape, a trivial misstep spells disaster.

Just as the space monster is about to retreat, the astronaut, overwhelmed by relief and succumbing to lunar flatulence, lets out a loud fart.

The unexpected noise reverberates through the barren moon, immediately catching the monster's attention.

The creature spins around, and with a terrifying roar, its eyes zero in on the astronaut's hiding spot.

Amidst this unexpected twist, the commercial ends abruptly, with a hilariously anticlimactic tagline appearing on the screen that reads 'Haynes beans – not for astronauts!'

It's a beautifully crafted punchline that ties together the entire narrative, leaving viewers both amused and astonished.

So as I recount this narrative, I hope it has spurred a release of endorphins within you—widely recognized as the 'happiness drug.'

Endorphins are your body's natural painkillers, produced in response to stress or discomfort.

However, their role extends beyond just pain relief.

As is the case here, these neurochemicals also contribute to feelings of pleasure and joy, often evoked by laughter.

Endorphins create a sense of happiness and relaxation, but their influence doesn't end there either.

They enhance focus, promote creativity, and induce an overall sense of positivity, a cocktail of effects that any storyteller or presenter would strive to generate in their audience.

While vastly different, these stories hold the same intrinsic value: they show how we can manipulate brain chemistry to capture attention, evoke emotion, and entertain our audiences.

Whether it's dopamine's influence on focus and concentration, oxytocin's role in fostering empathy and connection, or the joy-inducing effects of endorphins, each story, each commercial, has successfully engaged your brain uniquely and impactfully.

So, the next time you set out to create a narrative, be it a simple story, a presentation, or a marketing pitch, remember the power of storytelling and how it can 'drug' your audience's brain in a good way.

And now that we have waded into the intriguing world of neurotransmitters, experiencing their respective roles in amplifying our engagement with narratives, it's the perfect moment to introduce you to a delightful concoction known as the "Angel's cocktail".

This term, eloquently coined by the distinguished author and public speaker JP Philips, represents the fascinating blend of chemicals, specifically dopamine, oxytocin, and endorphins, triggered within us through expert storytelling.

And whilst we used the three commercials to isolate and illustrate the roles of each neurotransmitter in storytelling, this was essentially a pedagogical tool.

In practice, the effectiveness of great storytelling lies not in the isolated action of one chemical but in the holistic mix of all three, a whole symphony of the 'Angels cocktail.'

Recall the launch story we first explored.

Though it primarily stimulated the release of dopamine, encouraging focus and anticipation, it simultaneously triggered a release of endorphins and oxytocin, the latter experienced the challenges and triumphs of the team as they navigated through the roller-coaster ride of data-driven changes, we were touched by the camaraderie and resilience displayed, thereby inducing feelings of empathy and shared accomplishment.

Similarly, the second narrative, the 'Reader,' may have predominantly invoked oxytocin, fostering empathy and connection, yet it didn't fall short in delivering a good dose of dopamine and endorphins.

As we eagerly awaited the story's unravelling, a sense of suspense kept us on the edge of our seats while lighter, heart-warming moments peppered throughout brought smiles to our faces.

And finally, the 'Astronaut,' despite primarily targeting our endorphins with its cheeky humour, skilfully interspersed moments that provoked dopamine release.

The anticipation of the astronaut's fate and a shared understanding of the astronaut's predicament undoubtedly resonated with anyone who has ever enjoyed a hearty serving of baked beans, triggering a rush of oxytocin.

That, my friends, is the elegance and power of storytelling - a powerful tool that weaves a tapestry of emotions, experiences, and connections underpinned by the very physiology of our brains.

This combination, this 'Angel's cocktail', makes stories incredibly impactful, memorable, and integral to our life experiences.

In the later segments of this book, I will delve deeper into how you can harness this science to craft an irresistible narrative, whether for a business presentation, a public speech, or a casual conversation.

I will also introduce you to the darker twin of the 'Angel's cocktail,' ominously known as the 'Devil's cocktail.'

As the name suggests, it represents the antithesis of the uplifting blend we've been exploring, the nefarious effects of poor storytelling.

But before we delve into the shadows, let's continue our journey in the realm of light where our next question beckons us:

What constitutes a great story, and how can you become a proficient raconteur?

Let's explore that together in the next chapter of this book.

Chapter three
Art

The greatest art in the world is the art of storytelling.

Cecil B Demille - filmmaker

While we often celebrate creative minds for their ability to "think outside the box," a phrase that has embedded itself deeply in our cultural vocabulary, it may be a surprise that this isn't necessarily the cornerstone of great storytelling.

It's a common assumption to label extraordinary storytellers such as J.R.R Tolkien, Stephen King, Quentin Tarantino, and countless others as individuals who excel at transcending traditional boundaries.

However, I'm here to share an intriguing piece of insight, a revelation that might challenge your preconceptions - and no, this isn't a piece of 'fake news.'

Contrary to what you might think, the world's most acclaimed storytellers operate within a particular 'box,' a specific structure.

And here's the kicker, this 'box' is consistent across almost all successful narratives.

Before you conclude that I might have lost my marbles, let me share four simple yet profound words: "Once Upon a Time."

These are some of the earliest coherent words you heard as a child, the magical incantation that transported you to the realm of fantastical stories.

Yet, you may not realize that these words signify the opening of a universally recognized narrative structure known as the 'story spine.'

If the term' story spine' sounds alien to you, do not fret. Although the name might not be familiar, you've undoubtedly experienced it countless times.

This may seem entirely theoretical or foreign, so I shall now illustrate this concept with a real-life example to help solidify your understanding.

The example I will use is a classic Pixar film, "Monsters, Inc.," a personal favourite of mine and an all-time hit with my daughter Hollie during her younger years.

The film "Monsters, Inc." runs for one hour and thirty-six minutes.

And while every one of the ninety-six minutes offers a delightful blend of entertainment, I will distil this feature film into the story spine structure to demonstrate its utility.

So, let's begin.

"Once upon a time, a parallel world inhabited by monsters existed."

"And every day, these monsters relied on scaring human children to generate their world's power supply.

However, they faced a growing energy crisis as children became increasingly difficult to scare."

"Until one day, they stumbled upon the surprising discovery that children's laughter could generate far more energy than their screams."

"And because of that, they ceased their frightful tactics and instead sought methods to make children laugh."

"And because of that, they could produce significantly more energy with much less effort."

"And because of that, they managed to resolve their looming energy crisis."

"Until finally, they had more than enough power to sustain their world, and there were no more frightened children."

"And ever since then, the world of monsters has been filled with the sounds of cheerful, laughter-filled children."

So, as you can see, a feature film that lasts over ninety minutes can revolve around this simple, compact framework and this simplicity, combined with effective execution, can be the secret sauce for successful storytelling.

While the concept of the story spine might initially invoke images of whimsical fairy tales or engaging Pixar films, its influence extends far beyond these realms.

It doesn't solely occupy the enchanting world of enchanted forests, magical creatures, or animated characters overcoming enormous obstacles.

Instead, it is a ubiquitous element, a tool that writers and storytellers across various platforms utilize to craft compelling narratives.

Take a moment to consider a broader spectrum of storytelling mediums.

Think of famous novels that have left an indelible imprint on literature and readers' hearts alike, blockbuster films that have swept viewers off their feet with their captivating plots, or even addictive T.V. series that keep audiences hooked episode after episode, season after season.

While diverse in their format and audience, each of these storytelling platforms shares a common thread - a successful narrative structure.

And often, if you were to dissect these popular narratives, you would find that the story spine serves as their skeletal framework, the backbone that supports their plot, characters, and themes.

The story spine in these narratives gives rise to an engaging beginning that piques interest, a development phase that builds tension, a climax that leaves the audience at the edge of their seats, and a resolution that brings a satisfying conclusion.

This simple yet effective structure helps create a captivating journey that the audience embarks on along with the characters.

It's the driving force behind the page-turning quality of a beloved novel, the nail-biting suspense of a blockbuster film, and the "just one more episode" allure of a binge-worthy T.V. series.

Therefore, it's vital to recognize and appreciate the versatility and universality of the story spine.

It's more than just a storytelling tool for fairy tales or children's films.

It's a critical component that breathes life into narratives across genres and mediums.

The story spine is at the heart of storytelling, underscoring the narratives that entertain, inspire, and stay with us long after we've closed the book, left the theatre, or turned off the television.

For instance, let's consider the iconic 1975 thriller, "Jaws", and use the same story spine structure to break down the plot of this legendary thriller.

"Once upon a time," in Amity Island, a small, peaceful beach town, life revolved around the summer tourist season.

"And every day," locals and tourists enjoyed the sunny beaches and calm ocean waves, with the local police chief, Martin Brody, ensuring everyone's safety.

"Until one day," an unsuspecting swimmer was brutally attacked and killed by a massive, unseen creature from the depths.

"And because of that," the town was thrown into panic and chaos.

Despite pressure from local businesses to downplay the incident, Brody closed the beaches.

"And because of that," tensions rose.

When the predator struck again, Brody was compelled to hire a professional shark hunter, Quint, and a marine biologist, Matt Hooper, to hunt down and kill the shark.

"And because of that," the trio embarked on a dangerous journey on Quint's boat, the Orca.

The hunt proved gruelling, testing their skills, bravery, and sanity.

"Until finally," after a dramatic and deadly confrontation, Brody killed the shark, ending its reign of terror.

"And ever since then," the waters around Amity Island returned to their peaceful state, but with a newfound respect and wariness of what lurks beneath the surface.

So, even in the suspenseful, horror-tinged narrative of "Jaws," the story spine plays out, highlighting its universal applicability across genres and mediums.

And the story spine also governs the world of literature with the same iron fist.

For example, the epic novel Lord of the Rings by British author J.R.R. (John Ronald Reuel) Tolkien is not usually noted for its conciseness. Still, by applying the story spine, you can summarise it in less than a single page.

Once upon a time, a peaceful hobbit named Frodo Baggins lived in the Shire in Middle earth.

And every day, he would live a simple life full of comfort and quiet.

Until one day, his life was turned upside down when he inherited a mysterious ring from his eccentric uncle, Bilbo Baggins.

And because of that, he learned the Ring was the One Ring, the most potent and dangerous Middle-earth artefact created by the Dark Lord Sauron.

If Sauron were to regain the Ring, Middle earth would be plunged into eternal darkness.

And because of that, Frodo, with a fellowship including Gandalf the wizard, Legolas the elf, Gimli the dwarf, and Aragorn the ranger, set out on a quest to destroy the Ring in the fires of Mount Doom where it was created.

And because of that, they faced countless perils, from monstrous creatures like orcs and Ringwraiths to the treachery of Gollum, the former ring-bearer corrupted by the Ring's power.

Until finally, despite all odds, Frodo and his loyal friend Sam reached Mount Doom.

With Gollum's unintended help, the Ring was destroyed, defeating Sauron and his forces.

And ever since then, the world of Middle earth was free from the threat of the Ring.

Though Frodo was forever changed by his journey, he helped to bring about an era of peace and freedom.

So, as you can see, the realm in which the narrative power of the story spine extends is vast, more expansive than we initially perceive.

It stretches its influence across written tales and visual storytelling mediums like movies and T.V. shows and beautifully permeates the world of music.

Not just any music, though, but good music – music that captivates the listeners, taking them on an auditory journey, leaving them moved and inspired.

That might prompt you to wonder if the principle of the story spine could be used to encapsulate the works of contemporary pop artists like Justin Bieber or Little Mix.

While their music undeniably resonates with a vast audience and has a significant cultural impact, the concept of a narrative story spine might need to be revised in their catchy tunes and rhythmic beats.

The repetition of lyrics, the focus on infectious melodies, and the inclusion of bridge sections that don't necessarily progress the narrative could make it challenging to identify a clear, linear story spine in such works.

But this isn't to say it's impossible – music, after all, is a highly subjective art form that can be interpreted in countless ways and more of this in a minute.

But first, let's focus on what might be considered more established song writing.

When we look at some of the timeless classics, the application of the story spine becomes apparent, often driving the song's core narrative.

A perfect example is the iconic "Space Oddity," penned by the late and extraordinary David Bowie.

This piece isn't just a song; it's an auditory narrative that transports listeners into a tale unfolding in the infinity of space.

"Space Oddity" is more than just a tune; it's a narrative masterpiece, a journey, a chronicle set against the backdrop of the cosmos.

Each lyric, each note contributes to the unfolding of a story, from the take-off of the astronaut Major Tom to his solitary journey through the silent void of space.

The story spine governs this narrative, driving the song's plot, creating anticipation, and ultimately leaving the listeners in contemplation.

So then let's explore how "Space Oddity" exemplifies the story spine in music.

Once upon a time, there was an astronaut named Major Tom.

And every day, he embarked on daring space missions to explore the unknown, and each journey was filled with excitement and anticipation.

Until one day, as he floated in the vastness of space, he felt a mix of awe and isolation, and as his mission progressed, communication became increasingly difficult.

Until, in a pivotal moment, Major Tom lost contact with Ground Control, leaving him adrift and alone in the vastness of space

And because of that, he started to feel a sense of detachment and loneliness.

And because of that, a new emotion of fear also entered his mind.

And because of that, facing the uncertainty of his fate, he pondered the significance of his life and actions.

Until finally, Major Tom accepted the inevitability of his situation and embraced his destiny and the idea of floating in space indefinitely.

And ever since, he has looked down on the earth, happy in his fate, as told in his later hit, ashes to ashes.

With his poetic lyrics and compelling narratives, David Bowie has crafted songs beyond mere melodies and harmonies; they are stories encapsulated within music.

His song writing prowess and unique sound have left an indelible impact on music and beyond.

Bowie's songs, such as the iconic "Space Oddity," stand as testaments to the art of storytelling in music.

They follow a distinct narrative structure, leading listeners through events, evoking emotions and painting vivid pictures through his carefully chosen words. His songs brilliantly illustrate the application of the story spine in music.

Yet, whilst I carry a deep-rooted personal preference for the exquisite creative writings of the legendary artist Mr David Bowie, it's undeniable that the essence of storytelling and the application of the story spine can extend to contemporary songwriters, including pop sensations like Justin Bieber, whom I mentioned earlier.

Whether by design, accident, or subconscious exposure to the story spine from an early age, these more modern and contemporary artists employ it in their creative endeavours.

Despite the different genres, styles, and generations, the fundamental principle of storytelling prevails in their music too.

Bieber, known for his catchy tunes and heartfelt lyrics, also uses the narrative structure to drive the story of his songs, whether it's about love, heartbreak, or self-discovery.

In Bieber's music, you can still discern the structure of a story spine, though it may seem less explicit, or complex compared to Bowie's compositions.
Take a song like "Love Yourself," for example.

Once upon a time: There was a young man deeply in love with a woman.

Every day: She would tell him that he should change to fit her ideal of a perfect partner.
But one day: He realized that her criticisms were rooted in her insecurities and lack of self-love.

Because of that: He started to question the validity of her objections and the overall health of their relationship.

Because of that, He understood that he shouldn't change who he is just to fit someone else's ideals.

Because of that: He decided to break up with her, recognizing that the relationship was damaging his self-worth.

Until finally: He left her, suggesting she should take some time to love herself before entering a relationship with someone else.

The story spine is evident here, and it helps chronicle the journey of a young man in a toxic relationship, going through a series of events that led him to self-realization and, eventually, self-love.

The narrative progression in the song aligns well with the story spine, making the piece a hit song and a straightforward narrative journey.

So, while I harbour an unshaken admiration for the creative genius of David Bowie, it's essential to acknowledge the storytelling present in modern pop music.

Even though the style, tone, and themes may differ vastly, the narrative essence that underlies their creations remains consistent, pointing to the universality of the story spine.

Whether it's the timeless classics of Bowie or the chart-topping hits of Bieber, the story spine is a constant, highlighting its permeating influence in the world of music storytelling.

And finally, if for no other reason than it upsets me to finish the segment on music with a focus on Justin Bieber, being far from one of his greatest fans, we can also see the story spine evident in another musical genre and one which has evolved, but remains consistent in popularity and practice over time, that of heavy metal music.

A genre that I also share a passion for, heavy metal, despite my late father insisting that it was just a lot of noise when I was a teenager, heavy metal, perhaps more than any musical genre, is deeply in love with the story spine in its format, and dare I say deeply dependent upon this too.

Picking as an example the 80's classic Living on a Prayer by Bon Jovi - we find a clear story spine of two working-class characters struggling to make ends meet but holding onto their love and faith to get through it.

Whilst turning the amplifier up to the legendary eleven, as infamously told in the legendary movie Spinal Tap, a movie that itself is governed by the story spine format, be it works by Iron Maiden or the pioneers of Thrash metal Metallica, we find the story spine evident in all the lyrical content they deliver.

As you can see, the genuinely remarkable attribute of the story spine is its universal applicability.

And what is more, whilst we often think of stories as just residing solely in the realm of fiction, of made-up characters and imagined worlds, stories are all around us.

They permeate every aspect of our lives, from the books we read to the movies we watch, the conversations we have and the experiences we share.

Stories are fundamental to how we understand and interact with the world, and the story spine, in turn, is essential to these stories.

Indeed, there is scarcely an element in our world that doesn't conform, in some way, to the rules of the story spine.

Its narrative structure extends beyond real-world scenarios, factual accounts, and professional environments.

Take, for instance, the world of work and business.

At first glance, you may wonder, "How can a story spine apply to a business setting?"

But when you delve deeper, you see the threads connecting the two.

Every product or service, every marketing campaign, every business strategy, in essence, tells a story.

These stories are about identifying a problem (the setup), devising a solution (the confrontation), and achieving success (the resolution).

They follow the same narrative progression outlined in the story's spine.

Furthermore, the story spine's application is more expansive than external business storytelling.

It also plays a crucial role in internal communications, leadership, and team building.

A well-structured narrative can convey strategic goals, drive organizational change, and foster a cohesive company culture.

So, while the story spine may have its roots in fiction, its branches extend into all aspects of our lives.

It underscores our shared narratives and experiences, providing a structure that makes sense of our world.

Whether crafting a fairy tale, analysing a blockbuster film, or strategizing a business plan, the story spine remains an invaluable tool, something eloquently summed up by Jean-

Luc Godard when he said, "Sometimes reality is too complex. Stories give it form."

Sage words indeed, and as we progress, we will delve deeper into this fascinating intersection of storytelling and real-world applications, exploring how the story spine manifests in professional settings and how businesses leverage this narrative structure to create compelling stories, a fascinating journey that goes beyond fiction, venturing into the world of facts, work, and business.

And of note is the role that the story spine plays in the emergence of new artificial intelligence (A.I.) tools.

Interestingly, crafting a story spine is no longer a task exclusive to human creativity and imagination as the new generation of A.I. engines has evolved to master this art, adding an intriguing dimension to storytelling.

Indeed, creating a story spine is a task that these A.I. systems excel at.

And this isn't a hypothetical claim; it's a statement based on concrete performance, although, I assure you, none of the previous examples I provided was generated with the assistance of such A.I. They remain purely products of human ingenuity, but should you find this intriguing and wish to explore it further, you can readily test this A.I. capability yourself, with the likes of ChatGPT and Google BARD.

Ask either of these A.I. systems to generate the story spine of any film, book, or song, and you might be surprised at their responses' accuracy, coherence, and creativity.

These A.I. engines understand the structure of the story spine and can apply it to various narrative forms effectively, demonstrating their capacity to emulate an essential aspect of human creativity.

But turning back to purely human endeavours with the story spine, whilst you might think that such a rigid framework would block creativity, clearly it does not.
When used to create your narratives, the story spine doesn't restrict creativity; instead, it offers a solid framework to guide the creative process.

It ensures that while your imagination soars, it keeps sight of the fundamental elements that make a story coherent and engaging.
Moreover, using the story spine as a springboard for your storytelling allows you to immerse yourself in what makes narratives tick.

The process deepens your understanding of story elements like character development, pacing, and the critical 'conflict-resolution' dynamics, enhancing your appreciation of storytelling in all its forms.

Thus, the true magic of the story spine is found not just in its capacity to both distil and condense existing tales but also in its ability to act as a catalyst for the birth of new stories, limited only by the expanse of one's imagination."

So, if that sounds enticing and exciting, then good because now I will navigate you through using the story spine in anger.

So hopefully, after delving into the intricacies, nuances, and profound capabilities of the story spine, I will have converted you, or perhaps even brainwashed you, though in the most positive sense of the word, to the extensive benefits of this narrative structure.

As we've explored, the story spine has the power to unlock profound human emotions, foster connections, and reveal the underlying truths in our existence.

The story spine is not just a tool for writers, filmmakers, or artists; it's a critical component of the world in which we live.

Our lives are woven with stories, filled with conflicts, climaxes, and resolutions, much like the arcs that unfold in a well-crafted story spine.

Whether we realise it or not, we naturally gravitate toward the rhythm of this structure, finding comfort and meaning in its familiar pattern.

It may seem like a simple concept, and it is and the beauty of it is anyone and everyone, regardless of age, background, or education, can learn to use this invaluable tool but also master its use.
It doesn't require specialised knowledge.

Instead, it rewards creativity, observation, and empathy, which we all possess to varying degrees.

And as I have alluded to earlier in this book, it is also something we all have previously learnt and been exposed to.

The challenge for many of us is that, over time, we have forgotten.

Worse still, we have wrongly been taught that its use has no place in the professional world.

Instead, as the world has grown more complex and complicated to navigate, we have been taught that confusing and not convincing people is the only appropriate strategy for a successful career in business.

So, with that firmly in mind, Let's do a bit of unlearning and some re-learning with a couple of simple exercises to reawaken your storytelling skills.

Let's begin this exciting and enlightening journey by first thinking about something familiar and cherished a favourite film, book, or song that resonates with you on a personal level.

This familiarity will help guide us as we delve into the intricacies of crafting the story spine.

The story spine is a wonderfully flexible and adaptable tool that allows creativity and individuality so that you may use as many or as few 'and because of that' elements as you need to tell the story.
The other key benefit of this approach is that it accommodates complexity without becoming overwhelming and the key is to focus on significant impacts or elements within the plot that propel the story forward.

So, for this exercise, I have allowed five in the structure below, but please feel free to adapt as needed for your chosen narrative.

And if you find yourself in a situation where you cannot physically write the story spine, perhaps due to a lack of writing equipment or current geography. In that case, that's not a barrier to success.

Simply doing so in your head is equally effective, mentally traversing the same narrative process.

Visualisation can be a powerful tool, and this mental exercise still enhances your understanding and ability regardless.

And this is not an academic exercise; it's an exploration, an adventure into the heart of storytelling.

It's an opportunity to unlock your creative potential and embrace the universal language of stories with no right or wrong answers.

So, if you are ready, take a moment to settle into this task. Breathe deeply, clear your mind, and connect with your chosen story.

Visualise the characters, the setting, and the emotions. Feel the rhythm of the narrative as it unfolds and write your account on the following page.

Once upon a time

And everyday

Until one day

And because of that (use only as many as you need)

And because of that

And because of that

And because of that

And because of that

Until finally

And ever since

So how did you find that?

Difficult? Easy?

Still, trying to figure it out?

Don't worry. Just as with many skills we learn in life, a lack of use makes our storytelling skills seem missing or alien, but trust me, it will all come flooding back in full after a few goes.

And as with many things in life, the one thing that makes it easier is practice. And then more practice.

It is that simple.

And if you are still wondering whether your story writing skills are any good (and trust me, they will be), you can always turn to artificial intelligence AI as referenced earlier.

Probably due to the sheer number of stories which it can reference, AI has an incredible ability to create a story spine of any film, book or song you ask of it, so to compare and contrast your story, just visit Google BARD or ChatGPT and prompt it to 'please write a simple story spine of the film/book/song (delete as applicable and insert the title.) and see what it comes up as a reference point for your handiwork.

And a tip, too, always say please when 'prompting', at the very least when the apocalyptic vision of AI and Skynet, as depicted in the Terminator films, comes to fruition; your good manners may prove of immense value!

So now we have carried a little story writing 101, as it were, using something familiar and exciting to you.

Together, we've taken a beloved film, book, or song and dissected it using the story spine, uncovering the essential elements that make it resonate powerfully with audiences.

This 101 was an important step, allowing us to see a well-crafted narrative's inner workings and understand how different parts interconnect to form a compelling whole.

But our journey is far from over, as it's just beginning.

Let's now move on to Storytelling 102, where the story spine becomes more than a tool for analysis.

It becomes a creative mechanism for your ideas and outputs, a springboard that will launch your imagination into uncharted territories.

This next phase is where the magic truly happens as no longer are we merely playing back the creativity of others, passively observing, and understanding.

We are stepping into the creation arena, wielding the story spine to shape our unique visions and give life to our innermost thoughts and feelings although the transition may feel daunting at first, after all, it's one thing to analyse a story but another to create one from scratch.

But fear not, though, for the story spine is here to guide us, providing a clear, logical framework that simplifies the complex task of storytelling.

Imagine a canvas, blank and full of possibilities. The story spine is like the underlying sketch, the lines and shapes that guide the painting, helping to define the composition and flow where your creativity is the colour, texture, and emotion that will bring the canvas to life.

These are the seeds of your story and with the story spine's guidance, you can nurture these seeds, allowing them to grow and intertwine, forming a rich, captivating narrative.

Consider this a call to action, an invitation to step beyond the boundaries of what you know and explore the vast landscape of what could be.

It's an opportunity to make connections, experiment, fail, learn, and grow. It's a chance to discover what you can create and what you can become as a fully paid storyteller.

"To do this, I will ask you to utilise the story spine again, but this time for creative means, venturing into a new realm of storytelling.

We will write a story about one of the five pictures I will share and describe, each providing a different landscape for your creativity to flourish.

These pictures are more than mere images on a screen or paper. They are doorways into unexplored worlds, each holding the promise of adventure, emotion, and discovery.

Each picture serves as a prompt, a starting point from which your creativity can take flight. Each is filled with questions, conflicts, characters, and themes, all waiting to be explored and understood, a canvas you can paint with words, using the story spine as your brush.

Picture 1:

Here we see a young boy on a skateboard standing atop a steep hill looking downwards.

What is the story that goes with this image?

Is it the start or end of the story?

Are we seeing a young Tony Hawke or a future skateboarding visionary, and what is the from-to that accompanies his journey?

Picture 2:

Here we see a child's toy car that has impacted the crash barrier, leading to its abandonment.

What?

Why?

Who?

These are all questions that leap into mind, so what is the story to satisfy our curiosity here?

Picture 3:

Here we see a modern-day office populated by a staff of dinosaurs.

What has happened here?

Is it a metaphor or even a parallel universe?

What is the story that will bring this to life?

Picture 4:

Upon first observation, picture four appears to be a Star Wars plastic toy.

However, under further examination, we see that it is Steve Wars, a galaxy where everyone is called Steve.

Why?

What?

Where does this galaxy exist, and how did it come into being - and why does it have its range of reasonably priced toys too? Your story will unveil the truth.

Picture 5:

Picture five shows a cat, but no ordinary cat, instead a cat dressed in Rambo combat gear and a headband.

Again, what is the story behind this image?

Is it the start or the end of his adventure, and what is that adventure itself?

Your account will enlighten us about the facts.

So as before, the task is simple.

From here, let the story spine guide you in building your narrative, helping you navigate the ebb and flow of the plot, the cause and effect that drive the story forward.

Remember to make the story spine your own, adapting it as needed, making it flexible and responsive to your creative instincts.

This exercise is not just about constructing a story; it's about rediscovering something dormant within and offering a unique lens of your experience and creativity.

And to illustrate how a story about one of the above might look before you begin, here is my story about picture number two as both a guide and a source of inspiration.

Once upon a time, a little boy loved racing cars.

And every day, he would drive around his yard making engine noises in his Little Tikes car.

Until one day, he decided to go further afield and headed to the highway. Sadly, that day it didn't end well – and he hit the barrier – but his need for speed was set.

And because of that, his parents decided to buy him a go-kart.

And because of that, he started to race them and win.

And because of that, he started to get noticed by a gentleman called Ron Dennis.

And because of that, he worked his way up the ranks.

Until finally, one day, he became the Formula 1 world champion.

And ever since, he has continued to dominate the sport.

And the boy's name?

Lewis. Lewis Hamilton.

The seven times Formula 1 world champion.

So now it is your turn to write a story.

Take a deep breath, clear your mind, and allow the pictures to inspire you. Let your imagination wander, and trust in the process.

With the story spine as your companion and your creativity as your guide, you are ready to embark on this remarkable journey and remember, once again, that this is not an academic endeavour.

There are no right or wrong answers. Instead, it is about the joy of creation and the power of storytelling.

(Please note once again I have included five, and because of that, however, as before, feel free to use as many as you need for your story.)

Once upon a time

And everyday

Until one day

And because of that

And because of that

And because of that

And because of that

And because of that

Until finally

And ever since

So how did you find that?

As before, was it difficult?

Easy?

Still, trying to figure it out?

But wasn't it also fun, liberating, something you hadn't thought you could do?

And that is not only the power of the story spine but also its joy.

When embraced and used as intended, it allows anyone and everyone to be super creative and deliver narratives guaranteed to surprise and delight.

And what is more, those who often protest the loudest that they are not creative in any shape or form often produce the best and brightest stories thanks to their new friend, the story spine.

"But as I alluded to earlier, the power of the story spine is not restricted to the world of fiction.

Its applicability extends beyond tales of fantasy and adventure, reaching into our daily lives and the practical, tangible world.

In the world of facts, it is equally powerful when applied to the world of work.

Consider the variety and complexity of tasks, projects, and ideas in the working world.

Every day, individuals and teams are tasked with solving problems, generating new ideas, communicating complex information, and making critical decisions and in doing this the story spine offers an invaluable tool to help navigate these challenges.

In a business or professional environment, the story spine can structure presentations, outline strategies, communicate vision, and drive innovation.

It provides a clear and compelling framework that can turn abstract concepts into relatable narratives, making complex ideas more digestible and engaging.

Imagine utilising the story spine to articulate a company's mission, weaving the various elements into a cohesive story that resonates with employees and stakeholders alike.

It becomes more than a mere statement; it evolves into a narrative people can connect with, believe in, and be motivated by.

Or consider how the story spine can be used in product development.

By mapping out the user's journey, identifying the challenges they face, and articulating how a product or service can provide solutions, the story spine transforms a set of features and benefits into a compelling narrative that speaks directly to the customer's needs and desires.

In project management, the story spine can serve as a roadmap, guiding teams through the project stages and highlighting the cause-and-effect relationships that define the path to success. It encourages a broader perspective, prompting team members to think about the why and how, not just the what.

But the applications of the story spine in the professional world are not confined to these examples. Its flexibility and universality mean it can be adapted to virtually any context, challenge, or opportunity.

From marketing and sales to leadership and team building, from research and analysis to creativity and problem-solving, the story spine can be a powerful ally.

It's a bridge between logic and emotion, analysis and intuition, theory, and practice.

It recognises the human need for connection, for meaning, for story.

It acknowledges that we are not just rational beings processing information but also emotional beings seeking understanding, empathy, and inspiration.

The story spine is, therefore, more than a tool; it's a philosophy, a way of approaching the world that recognises the interconnectedness of all things, the underlying patterns that shape our experiences, and the narratives that give our lives meaning.

In embracing the story spine, we acknowledge that stories are not just entertainment but a fundamental part of the human experience.

They shape our thoughts, our actions, our relationships, our identities. They are the fabric of our culture, our organisations, our communities.

In the world of work, as in life, the story spine offers a path to greater understanding, creativity, collaboration, and success.

It's a testament to the timeless power of storytelling, a power that transcends boundaries, disciplines, and generations. It's a reminder that no matter where we are or what we do, we are all, in essence, storytellers, weaving narratives that define, inspire, and enrich our lives.

To quote Margaret Atwood, author of The Handmaid's Tale, who once wrote, "You're never going to kill storytelling because it's built in the human plan. We come with it."

And if all that sounds too Utopian or a little too made-up, then let me finish this chapter with my personal experience on the benefits of embracing the story in the world of work and why I believe so much in its daily use.

Many years ago, I worked for IPG, one of the more significant advertising holding companies, like my current employer, WPP.

And it was whilst there that I was introduced to the story spine myself.

Following an eventful training course, held in a mock castle somewhere outside of New York, itself worthy of a story spine I am sure, we were challenged to apply it directly to the world of work.

The challenge was simple but significant too.

We were challenged to write and share our business plans using the story spine format.

Crazy. Scary, with a healthy dose of what the?!...it didn't take long to realise this plan's genius.

It meant we had to assess and outline where we were. Define and describe where we wanted to go, and in so doing, find a clearly defined from-to.

And to get there, we had to find what we needed to change, connecting things with our 'because of that' to define the change we would bring.

And not just that, but we soon realised something else too.

Our plans were now written on a short single page and in a format that embraced simplicity too.

And these were plans that could be shared and understood by all and where there was nowhere to hide.

And not only that, but they also became our means of financial reward too, where story fiction becoming business fact was now how we were assessed.

Absolute genius and, for me, life-changing in the way I saw the world, and a world in which, to quote an old AOL colleague of mine, Arianna Huffington (founder of the Huffington Post), a world in which, "People think in stories, not statistics, and marketers need to be master storytellers."

Chapter four
Application

Stories constitute the single most powerful weapon in a leader's arsenal.

Dr Howard Gardner, Professor Harvard University

Without the villains, James Bond would undoubtedly be more a case of James Bland, as from the mercurial Jaws through to Blofeld and the more recent Raoul Silva, the ubiquitous bond villains are pivotal to the story and one that, without fail, is built around them.

And whether it is James Bond, Lord of the Rings or a Clint Eastwood Western of old, it is a simple fact, yet one worth exploring a little deeper, that most good stories, especially those containing a clear hero or heroine, also benefit immensely from having a villain.

This dynamic relationship between the protagonist and the antagonist is more than just a plot device; it's a fundamental structure that resonates with human psychology and how we perceive the world.

The presence of a villain in a story serves multiple purposes.

First and foremost, it provides conflict, the essential engine that drives the plot forward.

Conflict is at the heart of any gripping tale, creating tension, challenges, and obstacles the hero must overcome.

Without the villain, the hero's journey would lack direction, urgency, and drama.

There would be no mountain to climb, no dragon to slay, no wrong to the right.

But the role of the villain goes beyond mere conflict.

It is a foil to the hero, reflecting and contrasting their qualities, values, and motivations.

The villain challenges the hero's beliefs, tests their resolve, and often forces them to confront their weaknesses and fears.

This interaction between hero and villain adds complexity and depth to both characters, making them more relatable and compelling.

The villain can also serve as a symbol or metaphor, representing broader themes or societal issues.

They might embody greed, power, corruption, or other negative traits the story seeks to critique or explore.

In this way, the villain becomes more than a character; they become a manifestation of ideas, a vehicle through which the story can engage with moral, philosophical, and cultural questions.

Furthermore, the existence of a villain often prompts the audience to reflect on the nature of good and evil, right, and wrong.

It provokes questions about morality, ethics, and human nature.

What makes someone a villain?

What drives them to act in malicious ways?

How fine is the line between hero and villain, and how easily can one cross it?

These questions add philosophical weight to the story, elevating it beyond mere entertainment.

The relationship between hero and villain can also reveal insights into the cultural and historical context of the story.

Different cultures, eras, and societies have other notions of villainy, reflecting their values, fears, and aspirations.

By analysing the portrayal of villains in various stories, one can gain valuable insights into the collective psyche of a community or era.

In summary, the presence of a villain in a story is far from a simplistic or superficial element.

It is a multifaceted and essential component of the narrative's richness, depth, and universality.

It is a testament to the timeless wisdom and craftsmanship of storytellers throughout history that this relationship between hero and villain continues to captivate and inspire.

And whilst the above exploration of the role of villainy in storytelling establishes the importance of such characters in stories themselves, what is also of great significance is that storytelling itself has its villain, out to disrupt and destroy and one which often hides in plain sight.

To help illustrate this, at this stage, we shall return to the storytelling experiment approach, which I employed earlier in this book to show the chemical effects of great storytelling on our human bodies.

And sticking to my earlier use of advertisements as a mechanism to do this, I shall turn to the country of Japan, home to some of the most bizarre advertisements of all time, this one being no exceptions, to deliver our chemistry-laden experiment.

The advertisement in question is, in fact, one for tyres, those circular back items essential to the modern motor car.

However, you would be very hard-pressed to establish this once the brand is revealed at the end of the commercial.

Once again, as before, through the wonders of modern technology and the ubiquitous QR code, you can experience the commercial by scanning the one on the next page, but once again, for those not presently in possession of a mobile device or for those that do not believe in QR codes, I will also describe the commercial as it unfolds in word.

'GHOST'

Scan to watch

So, the commercial begins at night, shot from within the confines of a vehicle and depicts a journey along a snow-covered road, but before we even get to this point, the commercial starts with a warning message urging caution and stating that this commercial is not for the faint of heart.

Anyway, back to the commercial, and as we traverse forwards down the dark narrow, snow-covered road, after about five seconds in the distance, we suddenly see what appears to be a figure of a girl dressed in a white dress.

The car comes to a halt, and the girl appears to remain there, fixed to the spot several metres, if not more, in front of the vehicle.

Suddenly, and shockingly we see the girl's ghost-like face appear against the windscreen, sparking panic, at least for our erstwhile camera operator, and resulting in frantic efforts to escape by reversing back up the snow-covered road in haste.

We then cut to a close-up of the seemingly undead girl holding a laptop. (Well, it is the twenty-first century, and everyone is now online, even the undead, it would seem.)

On the screen, we see a message written in Japanese, which, given I sadly do not speak, urges them to buy new tyres or perhaps invest in some winter ones, given the snow-laden location.

Finally, it cuts to the end frame, where we learn it is for Auto way Tyres and shows their website to visit, assuming it is not currently unavailable due to too many visits from the undead.

So bizarre as this commercial is, the purpose of showing it was to deliver you a small dose of two chemicals, adrenaline, and cortisol.

Adrenaline is a hormone and neurotransmitter that plays a crucial role in the fight-or-flight response by increasing blood flow to muscles, pupil dilation response, and blood sugar level.

When adrenaline is released, it increases heart rate, blood pressure, and respiratory rate, preparing the body for a rapid response to a threat.

It can lead to Anxiety and nervousness and is often associated with intense emotions, primarily fear.

Cortisol is a steroid hormone produced by the adrenal cortex, and it helps regulate a wide range of processes throughout the body, including metabolism and the immune response.

It also has a significant role in helping the body respond to stress.

Like adrenaline, it plays a role in the fight-or-flight response, increasing glucose in the bloodstream and enhancing the brain's use of glucose.

It also curtails functions that would be nonessential in a fight-or-flight situation.

Combined, these two chemicals increase Anxiety and stress, as already highlighted, but also make you more irritable and critical, not to mention constraining creativity and the ability for memory-related tasks.

It is something that JP Philips, who you will recall, coined the phrase the Angels Cocktail for the combination of Dopamine, Oxytocin and Endorphins, termed the 'Devils Cocktail', given its opposite role in chemically delivered storytelling. As you have just experienced, these chemicals can be induced through fear, shock, and uncertainty.

Now, at this juncture, I should point out that if our storytelling goal is one grounded in the horror genre, then this is precisely the reaction we wish to elicit, and, indeed, any horror film worthy of the moniker must, by design do this.

Fear, Anxiety, lack of memory, tunnel vision and so forth are all the things we wish to induce if we aim to be the literary equivalent of Stephen king or the cinematic equivalent of Hitchcock.

However, sadly in the world of work and business, this is only generally something we seek to achieve if we want to decrease our customer base or favourability amongst our esteemed colleagues.

Yet sadly, in the world of work, there is also a fourth method by which you can induce the release of these chemicals: through, to put it crudely, shit PowerPoint and presentations.

And it is a method which is growing exponentially in popularity by the day, if, in fact, not by the hour.

It is a sad fact, but not perhaps for its inventor, that the only way we can convey and share information and stories in today's modern business world is through creating PowerPoint presentations, and, often, appallingly bad PowerPoint presentations.

This observation raises questions, concerns, and even frustrations about the evolution of communication within professional environments.

Once upon a time, business communication was characterized by face-to-face discussions, handwritten letters, and carefully crafted speeches.

It thrived on personal connection, thoughtful engagement, and balancing verbal and non-verbal cues.

Today, however, the landscape has shifted dramatically, and PowerPoint has become synonymous with professional presentations.

The pervasiveness of PowerPoint in business culture is a testament to its utility.

It allows for the structured presentation of complex information, facilitates visual engagement, and supports a wide range of multimedia elements.

Its accessibility and apparent ease of use have made it the go-to tool for executives, managers, marketers, educators, and even students.

But this widespread adoption has come at a cost.

The true power of storytelling, the ability to connect emotionally, inspire action, and foster deep understanding, often must be noticed in a sea of bullet points, confusing charts, and generic templates.

What should be a tool to enhance communication frequently becomes a crutch, leading to oversimplification, confusion, and disengagement.

The art of crafting a bad PowerPoint presentation seems to have become as prevalent as the tool itself.

Common pitfalls include a lack of focus on narrative structure, overreliance on text, misuse of visuals, and a failure to consider the audience's needs.

These mistakes transform what could be a dynamic and engaging experience into a monotonous and often frustrating ordeal.

The irony is that PowerPoint was designed to facilitate communication, to make it more effective and engaging.

However, its misuse has led to a situation where it often hampers understanding and connection.

Instead of enhancing the sharing of ideas and stories, it becomes a barrier, filtering and distorting the message.

It is the "I know you cannot read it, but I have added the spreadsheet anyway" PowerPoint chart.

The complex wiring diagram chart that you are certain contains the plans for a Saturn IV rocket or the like.

The three PowerPoint charts were pasted into one in a cunning attempt to reduce the number of slides chart.

Or finally, the one where the carefully selected picture is then hidden by a thousand words and bullet points chart.

Now in my more Utopian moments, I dream of a world without PowerPoint, or for that matter, Keynote.

Indeed, later in this book, I will explore ways we can at least start that journey.

However, with Utopia off the table for now, in the remainder of this book, I will now explore how to use what we have covered so far in this book along with some simple rules for writing a presentation, which, if you adhere to them should allow you to become a master of storytelling when it comes to writing and giving that killer presentation.

Think of it as the Q-branch of presentation writing, the gifts and gadgets that will help you succeed, even when in a tight squeeze.

And please note the use of the word presentation.

A presentation is a very different animal from a document or a detailed spreadsheet of information.

It is inherently linked to the world of the story and where the intersection between stage and level are many and where the ability to manipulate your audience through chemistry of the good kind.

So, if you're ready, pay attention, as coming next are my ten essential techniques or even tricks if you will when be creating and giving a killer presentation and where you can ultimately exhibit your inner Bond to Bowie.

#1

<u>Begin with some Dinosaurs, Unicorns, and Time Travel</u>

It might seem entirely obvious, but the first thing that can make or break your presentation is the title itself.

Think about it.

The title of a presentation or lecture is more than just a simple tag; it's a powerful element that precedes face-to-face interaction.

This title is often seen or shared long before anyone enters the room.

As the first point of contact with potential listeners, the title is critical in communication.

It must do more than act as a functional description of the content.

It must also act as a lure, sparking curiosity and drawing people in.

The title must be carefully crafted to entice those who come across it and it must intrigue by hinting at something unexpected or promising an insightful experience.

It must inspire them by suggesting they will gain something valuable from attending. It should stir emotions, causing them to feel something significant, whether it's excitement, wonder, or even a bit of mystery.

And finally, it must motivate, making people feel compelled to come along and listen.

It's not just about informing; it's about engaging, attracting, and promising something that stands out from the everyday.

In many ways, the title sets the tone for the entire presentation.

It offers a glimpse into the speaker's creativity, approach, and level of thought and effort invested into the content.

In short, a well-chosen title can distinguish between a room filled with eager listeners and an empty one, the first step in a journey that you want others to take with you, and a means to administer your first dose of dopamine to an expectant audience.

Take, for example, the world of Cinema and motion pictures.

As we have explored already, these are all stories constrained and constructed within the rules of the story spine.

For example, the Film Jaws is a cinematic masterpiece we have already deconstructed with the story spine earlier in this book.

Upon its release to the public, it generated tremendous excitement and interest, no doubt in large part down to the title itself, Jaws and the iconic cinema poster that accompanied it of a giant shark looming below an unsuspecting swimmer.

Indeed, as an individual not yet in his teenage years at the time, it created a sense of intrigue, fear excitement, even if I had no chance of being allowed into the cinema to view it.

But imagine for a moment what would have happened had they decided to entitle this cinematic masterpiece with a more functional and less emotive title, say for the sake of argument, 'A film about a big fish.'

If that had been the case, I doubt that Jaws would have become the iconic film it did, nor would we have seen Jaws II and III hit the silver screen in the following years.

Switching genre entirely, take, for example, the movie 'Fear and Loathing in Las Vegas.'

The title oozes dopamine-laden intrigue and makes you want to know more.

Yet again, imagine if Terry Gilliam had decided to call his cinematic masterpiece by a more functional name, for example, 'A man goes to Las Vegas.' It doesn't have the same ring to it I am sure you will agree.

And what if Star Wars were entitled 'Some Men and a Few Robots in Space'.

Or imagine, God forbid, that the James Bond epic Skyfall had been named 'A house somewhere in Scotland just off the A9."

And it is the same for both books and. songs, with many cinematic masterpieces owing their title entirely to the book upon which they are based.

By now, you get my point.

The title you assign to your presentation has a critical role, which is as essential as what follows.

Yet when it comes to presentations, most people choose to go with entirely functional or descriptive titles, missing completely the opportunity to inspire, excite and intrigue, administering that first hit of dopamine.

'A presentation to." 'A presentation on'.

'Client X - Mid-year review.'

Boring all of them, and a huge opportunity missed to engage the audience.

This then begs the question of how to find a better, more inspiring, and dopamine-laden title for your presentation. Well, there are a few ways to tackle this.

One way is to use a from-to mechanism, which is as simple as it sounds.

Once the presentation is written, identify the overarching change or from-to within it and use this as the title.

And when doing so, you can also find a theme or narrative that is exciting and rooted in an engaging cultural reference or story.

For example, when I was asked to present about the world of data, a potentially dry and sleep-inducing subject for the unenlightened, it would be super easy to use a title such as 'A presentation on the future of data' or 'Effective use of data in business.'

Instead, I chose a title of 'From data death stars to Data Jedi' reflecting a critical point in my narrative that effective use of data relies more on the right people and skill sets (the Jedi) versus the accumulation of vast data sets in what I term data death stars.

And not only did this afford me what I would venture is a much more exciting and dopamine-laden title for my presentation, but it also allowed me a theme around which I could create my entire story and presentation from a visual perspective.

And should you not utilise a from-to format, then a similar thought process can be employed, as illustrated by another example from my presentation past library.

During the Covid-19 pandemic, I was asked to create a perspective on the emergence and evolution of streaming platforms along with a view on future evolution and whether Disney, as a new player, could topple the dominance of Netflix.

Again, it would have been straightforward to go with a title such as 'The future of digital streaming platforms' or 'Streaming now, next and future' although, on reflection, that last title is pretty good!

Instead, I went with the title of 'The Streaming Wars', an altogether more exciting title and one given the Disney connection, once again allowed me to play with a Star Wars-themed narrative and design format.

To conclude my considerations regarding the presentation title, I will now also address two questions I often get asked when speaking or training on this subject.

Firstly, I have been challenged when making these assertations that often the title of a presentation is already given and that, as such, there is no possibility of utilising something more exciting.

I have experienced this challenge several times, and it is a rule that whilst you can respect, you can also easily bend to your benefit and that of your expectant audience.

As a case in point, I was once asked to step in at the last minute to cover a presentation entitled 'How to accelerate growth through marketing transformation.'

Certainly not the most dopamine-inducing title, but one that sadly had already been conveyed in a printed invite and agenda.

So, my solution was simple.

I kept the title but as a sub-header to the more inspiring title of 'Dinosaur, Unicorns and Time travel', merging the two and, in so doing, merely bending the rules, not ignoring them entirely.

And if you were wondering as to why this title, then it was drawn from my theme, which highlighted that in a complex world which has changed from the world in which I started my communications career, the challenge had become one of how not to be a dinosaur, but rather a unicorn business which at the time was the aspiration of many.

And the final question I often get asked is whether you should start or end the construction of a presentation with the title.

The answer to that is short and straightforward.

It doesn't matter and largely depends on how you think.

Having the title or theme in my head is often helpful so I can expand the presentation's content.

It has also often allowed me to utilise a clear theme and style, as highlighted earlier with my Star Wars-themed stories.

However, I have also been known to do the opposite and bring my title into play at the end after completing the detailed content, so at the risk of being little or no help on this question,

I urge you to do what feels best for you.

Now armed with what is, hopefully, an inspiring, enticing, and exciting dopamine-laden presentation title, it is time to turn to our second presentation gadget, the agenda.

#2

Have no agenda.

So, your presentation now has a fantastic title that excites, intrigues, and inspires, delivering that all-important dopamine hit.

Again, it might be stating the obvious, but once you navigate your presentation title, the following essential component in setting up a successful presentation, before you even get to the content, is the contents or agenda slide.

This underrated aspect serves as more than just an itinerary of the journey you're about to embark on with your audience.

Instead, it's a beacon, a roadmap to the treasure that your presentation promises, and represents a golden opportunity to excite and intrigue the audience further and offer them specific waypoints to maintain their focus and attention.

Then, without even realising it, you snatch defeat from the jaws of victory with your next slide, the agenda, because this is often a secondary thought for most presenters.

This necessary evil lists the things to be covered with bullet points.

Beyond that, it has no further value or requirement for additional care or consideration.
Even more detrimental is the fact that by sticking to the conventional and unimaginative method of presenting the agenda, there is a considerable risk that you will undermine the hard work you put into formulating an attention-grabbing title.

By turning the schedule into a mundane list, the presenter might unwittingly establish a tone that is more likely to induce audience fatigue than pique their interest.

As a result, the presentation is seen as a task to be endured rather than an enriching experience to be relished.

So, if we accept the above to be accurate, it raises the question of what is an alternative means by which to share the content of your presentation and provide those essential waypoints for your audience.

As with many things in life and the world of good presentations, the answer lies in the number three.

A little later, I will expand on why three is meaningful and impactful beyond all others and why it is the magic number for presentations.

Still, if you humour me, I will first describe how to convey the agenda or presentation contents.

And as with most things that work exceptionally well, my method is straightforward.

And that is to use a chart bearing the headline of three things for today.

And as the title would suggest, I then play back the key three things I want my audience to look out for, the critical waypoints and, ultimately, to take away.

And focusing on the last one for a moment to ensure that these are indeed the three things that they take away from everything you subsequently present, then all you must do is reprise the chart at the end of your presentations, but with a slightly altered headline that reads three things from today.

This simple wordplay and trick, at the very least, ensure that should your audience have not listened to a single word you said, then at the end, they can at least understand what the noises you were making were in aid of.

Still, given you have designed and delivered it using the wisdom in this book, that is an improbable eventuality!

So next up, given that the advice is to constrain your agenda to just three key things, the question becomes, what are the three things you should utilise here?

Well, the rule I usually follow is this.

The first item is generally grounded in fact or factual. For example,

"We will save you X' or "How we can deliver X% of growth."

Of course, this can be adjusted to the audience, but even in the world I inhabit, advertising, someone will usually want to know to expect a hard commercial benefit to be evident in a presentation.

It also acts as a perfect antidote to anyone who doesn't like 'Fluff', as one of my favourite colleagues calls it, the storytelling side of things to offer a brief explanation.

And talking of antidotes, the second item for me can then act as an antidote to the factual or functional, and that is what I call the fascination and fun fact.

This presents a perfect opportunity to offer a little bit of excitement and intrigue and thinking back to our Angels cocktail from earlier in the book, a little bit of dopamine and endorphins too.

To offer a couple of real-world examples of how this works, many years ago,

I was involved in a series of pitch presentations to a large pharmaceutical company that, amongst other products, offered a range of mouthwashes for purchase.

Our strategic insight was good: people didn't care about mouthwash, but they certainly did care about their mouths and what it could do for them.

As such, the product received little positive coverage in this regard and, conversely, was subject to a lot of what I will call bizarre coverage in some quarters, including a lot of coverage around its ability to kill or repel the common mosquito.

This created several problems, not least that when people searched for the product, they found links to content posing this question, along with others which alarmingly spoke to its merit as an alcoholic beverage for the financially challenged.

The task, therefore, or at least as we saw it was to replace this content, which appeared when you searched for the product, with much more meaningful and relevant content and coverage relating to the wonders of your mouth and the importance, therefore, to care for it.

So, to introduce this and create intrigue in our agenda, our second point under three things for today was something along the lines of "Why a mosquito is the answer to supercharging your search." my apologies, as I cannot recall the exact line, but trust me it was undoubtedly a little sharper than that.

And it certainly worked, raising a wry smile and curiosity amongst the audience, which was highlighted when we got to the mosquito story within the content. "Now I get it" was one individual's remark, followed by "Very smart."

Not only that, but the same individual, who it turned out would be intending all the subsequent meetings, then took to alerting his colleagues to the upcoming mosquito when we shared the agenda, emphasised with a commentary of "Look out for the mosquito" and ensuring that his erstwhile colleagues, now subject to a small dose of dopamine were on high alert for when the mosquito buzzed in as it were.

And similarly, a few years later, when pitching to a large client in a highly restricted category, our second point was entitled, "Why Donald Trump is right when it comes to content."

I will expand on this story a little more later in the book, but for context here, the back story to this highly provocative proclamation, and one which raised many eyebrows in the room when unveiled, was that at the time, Mr Trump seeking election to the US Presidency, had realised that free speech, and particularly Twitter, now known as ElonX or something, to share content and engage in conversations free of advertising restrictions.

Our point was, therefore, a simple one: in a highly restricted category, a similar content-led strategy could work.

When we reached this waypoint in the presentation, it was called out by several in the audience and again reinforced with comments along the lines of "now we get it" and once again further comments of "very smart!"

And when it comes to the third thing to use under your three things for today, my usual approach here is to utilise something that is friendly or empathetic and will invoke a release of Oxytocin in your audience.

For example, this can include highlighting previous relationship highlights or intended future goals, using language such as 'why our partnership matters' or "Why we are the right partner for you."

The only watch out here is always to be sincere and authentic.

Too many saccharin-laden superlatives can negate this and quickly remove Oxytocin from your audience, not add it.

Now, of course, as with all things, these are helpful rules, but not rules that must be set in stone.

For one, sometimes reordering the above and leading with the last first is entirely appropriate.

Indeed, this can be a wise choice regarding the business re-pitch and see the friendly and factual lead over the fun or fascinating.

And sometimes the above is not appropriate at all.

But does this mean reverting to the sleep-inducing traditional bullet point agenda slide?

Not at all.

In this instance, my fallback approach is constructing my

agenda from the three W's:
Why?

What?

and Now or So What?

Why is where you set up the argument for, the why.

What is where you unveil the solution or approach.

And finally, Now What or So What, where you end on the action plan or benefits this will bring.

It also provides a simple, clean navigation approach, dividing your content into evident placeholders.

And in this role as a navigation aid, it can also quite comfortably be used along the three things for today by changing its title to agenda or contents and then adding the more intriguing three things slide straight afterwards and then again at the end, with the title changed to Three things from today as previously discussed.
So, there you have it.

You have an exciting, dopamine-laden presentation title slide and an agenda that further reinforces this, meaning your audience is fully attentive, expectant, and ready to hear your story.

And what better way to start your story than with a story itself, as I will now elaborate on.

#3

Start with a story.

So, it is time to get your presentation and carefully crafted story underway, and what better way to do so than using a smaller account or story within your overall one.

A tried and tested technique, it is one I have seen used by skilled presenters throughout the years, not to mention one that is a favourite of accomplished moviemakers.

And more alert of you will have noted that I started this book by asking you to view a short story on the history of James Bond using the QR code I invited you to scan.

Uttering the words, "Let's start with a story", is one of the best ways to begin a presentation, and the mere use of the term with disarm your audience away from expectations or a functional or factual representation (although by now they are hopefully expecting more) and to a place where their sub-conscious storytelling brain awakens.

So, what should your story be?

It can be anything, but I use a few rules or guidelines when employing this technique.

Firstly, it should be simple and short.

That might sound obvious, but it is there to support your deeper narrative or story and, therefore, should not burden it with its complexity nor distract your audience with too long a duration.

Secondly, it should be seen as an opportunity to give your audience another dose of the angels' cocktail, composed of dopamine, oxytocin, and endorphins, and therefore chemically connecting and bonding them to you as the presenter.

Thirdly, and this is stating the obvious a little, it should have a clear point to make and one that supports the main story.

And finally, conscious that I am breaking my usual rule of three (more on that later), it doesn't need to be constrained by a mere slide.

It can be a movie.

A picture that is supported by an anecdote or even an object, or even a short activity.

To elaborate on the last two, I will again give examples from my past presentations.

Several years ago, I joined a new agency, only to be presented within my first week with the news that one of their largest clients was unhappy with the current stage of things and, as such, had decided it should undergo a closed review of the business.

Benefiting from being new and unencumbered by any of the history or human relationships, I took it upon myself to dig into what lay behind this decision and found two clear themes.

Firstly, the relationship on both sides was suffering from what I would term cracks and fractures, leading to people viewing the greener grass on the other side and both sides blaming each other for the situation and neither willing nor able to say sorry meaningful way.

But secondly, behind these apparent cracks and fractures remained a value and hard-won expertise within the existing work and relationships that would be near impossible to replicate, at least in the short to medium term.

So how to navigate that first tough meeting with our client and the consultants charged with offering a means for mediation, and even more challenging, how to introduce that meeting correctly?

Step forward the story.

And in this case, a little story of Kintsugi.

For those unaware, Kintsugi is a traditional Japanese art form that involves repairing broken pottery using lacquer mixed with powdered gold, silver, or platinum.

Rather than hiding the cracks and imperfections, this technique emphasizes and celebrates them, treating the breaks as a unique part of the object's history.

The philosophy behind kintsugi speaks to embracing flaws and imperfections, and it is often seen as a metaphor for resilience, acceptance, and the ability to see beauty in the broken or imperfect.

And what better way to replay this story than by giving its recipients their unique piece of Kintsugi in the form of a bowl - an apology but not one that looked to the past or to attribute blame, but rather one that looked to the future and found the value in what had gone before.

This simple story, told with an object and grounded in culture, gave us the power to transform.

It drew a line under the past and sent a joint goal for us to make an already precious relationship even more valuable, something I am glad to say we were then able to do.

The second story involves a mobile phone, a pair of trainers and then, subsequently, some coffee beans, but more of those later.

The presentation was a pitch to a phone company.

The insight around which the story was built was that a smartphone was a unique product compared to most because it grew in value after its purchase by adding data and apps.

And if you think about it, it is true. Most items we buy lose value once unboxed. A mobile, not so much.

To bring this to life, the presentation started with a simple story based on a physical item, some rather lovely Gazelle trainers from our then-client Adidas.

It was also a great way to establish our youth credentials too, being the agency of record for Adidas, who we knew the prospective client much admired for their marketing efforts. Again, simplicity was vital, and after a setup along the lines of "let's start the story with something that you have but which most clients do not, including Adidas",

The previously untouched trainers were then unboxed and, in so doing, immediately devalued to act as proof to this introductory story.

A simple story to make a simple point, and it was one well-made and received.

Incidentally, the person responsible for the conception of this lovely little story, a good friend of mine who will remain nameless here, subsequently decided to employ the same tactic or at least logic in a future pitch for a coffee brand too.

This time a hand full of coffee beans were unveiled to the same story.

However, for reasons I needed to be fully updated about, the story didn't land as well on that occasion, and the pitch could have been more successful.

But that last occasion aside, through the first two anecdotes, you can understand how a simple story using an object can be a potent storytelling mechanism, especially in a pitch presentation, as can using any form of story to start, and in so doing providing your audience with a nice cocktail, an angel's cocktail of course!

But in the world of presentations, it would be fair to say that you are only as good as your last slide, and to that effect, I will share with you the only presentation rule that I never, ever will break and to find out what that is, read on!

#4

Think story, not slides.

Yet again, what I am about to say may seem obvious, but it's a principle that bears repeating, especially in presentation writing.

It's an axiom that, surprisingly, only some people constrain themselves by or, indeed, for that matter, seem to be aware of.

The rule is simple yet profoundly impactful: you should only attempt to make one point per slide.

This rule is a critical guidepost in presentations, whether in business, academia, or any other field where ideas must be conveyed clearly and conclusively.

But why is it so significant, and why is it so often overlooked or neglected?

The principle of one point per slide is rooted in the understanding of human cognition and the way we process information.

We live in an age of information overload, where attention spans are increasingly fragmented.

People are inundated with data, visuals, and narratives, competing for their focus. In such an environment, simplicity and clarity become paramount.

When a slide in a presentation tries to convey multiple points, it can lead to confusion, dilution of the main idea, and a loss of engagement from the audience.

The message becomes muddled, and the audience may need help to discern the key takeaway.

In contrast, focusing on one clear, well-articulated point per slide allows for a more streamlined and effective communication process.

This isn't merely a suggestion; it's a guideline backed by research in cognitive science.

Studies have shown that our brains are more adept at absorbing information when presented in bite-sized, digestible chunks.

By adhering to the one-point-per-slide rule, presenters can ensure that their audience follows along and retains and internalises the information being shared.

Yet, despite its apparent simplicity and the logic behind it, this rule is often ignored. But why?

The desire to pack as much information as possible into a presentation, especially when faced with time constraints, may be one reason.

It could also be down to a need for more awareness about human cognition and how our brains best absorb information.

Or it could also reflect a broader cultural shift towards multitasking and information saturation, where the tendency is to try to do more, say more, and show more, often at the expense of clarity and impact, where being loquacious in your content is seen as some badge of honour.

Yet, whilst all the above doubtless contribute to this in varying degrees, in my experience, the single biggest reason this happens is the number of slides or, instead, a limit on the number of charts a person can use.

If I had a pound or dollar every time, I heard phrases such as, "You only have ten minutes, so no more than ten slides, please." Or "Can you just create a ten slider", as I recently heard repeated on a project."

The truth is that the length of a story and the number of slides at best are mere casual bedfellows and, at worst, the most bitter of enemies.

Yet when it comes to presentation writing in the modern era, one dominated by PowerPoint, this obsession with the number of slides has often become all-consuming and detrimental to the art of storytelling and human communication through such mediums.

It has led to some extremely bizarre and entirely destructive behaviours being adopted as people battle to work within ten slides or less, focusing on this rather than the story they need to tell.

And central to this has become the emergence of the 'drost-slide' as I call it or sometimes also known as the lesser spotted infinity slide.

The Droste effect is a visual recursion phenomenon named after the Dutch cocoa company Droste.

It refers to an image that appears within itself, where a similar picture would realistically be expected to occur, creating an infinite loop in which the image within the image contains a more miniature copy of itself, and so on.

The term was coined based on the design of Droste's cocoa tin, which depicted a woman holding a tray with a cup of cocoa and the same tin with the same image.

The smaller image then contains an even smaller print, which theoretically continues into infinity.

The Droste effect is used in various art forms and can be created using mathematical principles or digital image manipulation.

Artists, photographers, and filmmakers have used it to create visually intriguing works.

When translated to PowerPoint, the Droste effect is easy to spot. It is the slide created by posting several other smaller slides within it.

Do you need to say four things but have been told only to use one slide? No problem, the Droste slide has your back!

But not only does this create something that visually looks complex and confusing and creates cerebral overload for the audience, but it also disregards that one sacred rule outlined earlier - making just one point per slide.

Imagine visiting a lovely Michelin-starred restaurant, tucked away in a picturesque corner of a charming city, where culinary dreams come alive.

When you step inside, you are greeted by an ambience that perfectly blends elegance and comfort with soft lighting, tasteful décor, and an inviting atmosphere that promises an unforgettable dining experience.

You are there to indulge in their renowned ten-course tasting menu, a gastronomic journey that promises to tantalise the senses.

As you settle into your seat, you are attended by a skilled Sommelier, an expert in wines, who presents you with an extensive wine list.

No ordinary selection but a carefully curated collection representing worldwide regions, each bottle a story, waiting to complement the symphony of flavours the chef has orchestrated.

The meal begins with a delicate amuse-bouche, a single bite that sets the tone for the evening. It's a masterful creation, bursting with flavours, teasing your palate, and leaving you eagerly anticipating what's to come.

The Sommelier gracefully pours the first wine, explaining its origin, unique characteristics, and why it pairs perfectly with the dish you are about to enjoy.

You take a sip, and the wine dances on your tongue, harmonising with the food in a way that transcends mere eating.

Each course is a revelation as the evening progresses, showcasing the chef's creativity, skill, and deep understanding of ingredients and taking you through a journey of textures, temperatures, and tastes that defy expectations.

Except they are not, because it is all served on the same plate at the same time, and the intricate selection of wines are all poured into one large glass for you to enjoy or not.

Or imagine arriving at a busy road junction, but thankfully one governed and carefully controlled by red and green traffic lights.

Then to your shock, red and green lights are illuminated together, leading to the inevitable car crash.

Now whilst both scenarios are fictional and very unlikely to exist in the real world, this is precisely the experience your audience undergoes when you break that one point per slide rule and fixate on slides, not the story.

And it is an experience that, sadly, audiences around the world experience almost daily, and one that need not be if people were to focus on telling their story in the time allocated instead.

Several years ago, I was invited to deliver a presentation at an event called innovation mecca in Oslo, the capital of Norway, and if you still need to visit, I urge you to try, as it is a beautiful city.

Now the format for the presentation was simple.

You were given ten minutes to deliver your content, with a timer counting down on a screen in clear view.

Once the timer reached zero, that was it, and your presentation visuals and sound would immediately cease, indicating the end of your presentation time.

Excited by this prospect, I created a story about the evolution of storytelling into story-living and story-making for the modern consumer.

I then sent all 130 slides by email to the event organiser in advance, as had been requested.

It then didn't take me long to receive a reply, "Thanks for the presentation, but we note you have 130 slides, and your slot is only allocated for 10 minutes maximum.'

More amused than annoyed at this response, I replied, "Great, I look forward to it, and yes, you are correct. The presentation is 130 slides long but is intended for the allocated time slot."

To avoid the monotony of the subsequent email exchanges that followed, I will fast forwards to tell you that the matter was settled through a simple bet.

If I could not deliver my content in the allocated time, I would suffer the ignominy of failing in my task and be expected to purchase drinks for the organisers after the event.

And to conclude the story, let's say that I enjoyed an excellent bottle of wine that evening with the organisers, but at their expense, not mine, having finished within the allotted time and with four seconds to spare.

So, the point here is clear, to focus on the story, not the slides, and in so doing, stick to the one golden rule that I will never break, make just one point per slide.

And alongside this, there are also a couple of related things to consider, which can further enhance your clarity.

Firstly, as well as making just one point per slide, add a further filter to see if it also delivers a clear insight and implication for your audience.

Again, this is common sense, but sometimes in the excitement of creating a presentation, style can overcome substance and the 'so what' test, as an old CEO of mine termed it, is forgotten.

Secondly, drop the bullet points.

No, seriously, drop them.

Not only do bullet points encourage making more than one point per slide, but they also promote adding content that is entirely unnecessary and protracted, as the quest becomes one of filling four or five bullet points rather than making your single point succinct and super sharp.

If you see a slide with two bullet points, it creates the illusion of being incomplete or lacking in content, but when removed, the effect reverses, and it sings and shouts simplicity and sharpness.

And finally, in the spirit of sharpness and making a single point per slide, think carefully before adding the presentation graph.

By design, although intended to visualise complex numerical information better, graphs still have a fundamental design flaw; although they simplify, they generally do not single out.

Even the greatest-looking graph must show more than one data point by nature of its form and function.

Therefore, you must ensure that the point you wish to make or share through the presentation graph is clear through either headline or highlighting.

If not, reconsider and search for a different means to convey your message.

And finally, whilst the single point per slide is a rule, I suggest you keep, there is one noticeable exception and one we have already explored, the contents and conclusion.

And for that, I have already suggested that you utilise the number three, which raises the question of why then three?

Something we will now explore in more detail.

#5

Three is the magic number.

We live in a world that, whether we know it or not, is composed of and governed by the number three.

Historically, many cultures and religions worldwide have significant associations with the number three, often attributing mystical or sacred meaning to it.

In Christianity, the number three holds a central place through the concept of the Holy Trinity, representing the Father, Son, and Holy Spirit.

These three distinct entities symbolise different aspects of the Divine, and their interrelationship has been a profound subject of theological study and worship.

The Trinity has been depicted in art, literature, and liturgy, reinforcing the concept's deep-rooted significance within the Christian faith.

Similarly, in Buddhism, the "Three Jewels" or "Triple Gem" comprise the Buddha, the Dharma (the teachings), and the Sangha (the community of monks and nuns).

These three aspects form the core of Buddhist belief and practice, where the Buddha represents the enlightened one, the Dharma is the path of teachings to attain enlightenment, and the Sangha embodies the community that follows the Dharma.

Devotees often recite their commitment to these Three Jewels in a formal practice known as "taking refuge," signifying their dedication to enlightenment.

In Hinduism, the number three resonates with the Trimurti, the three principal deities: Brahma the Creator, Vishnu the Preserver, and Shiva the Destroyer.

These gods symbolise the cyclical nature of existence, including creation, preservation, and destruction.

The ancient Celts also revered the number three, believing in its magical properties.

Triads or groups of three are a recurring motif in Celtic myths, and three-faced or three-headed figures have been discovered in archaeological sites.

In Chinese culture, the number three is considered lucky and associated with positive attributes.

The philosophy of Taoism speaks of the "Three Treasures" of humanity: Jing, Qi, and Shen, representing Essence, Energy, and Spirit.

Even beyond specific religious contexts, the number three appears in countless folktales, myths, and cultural practices.

The motif persists from the three wishes granted by a genie to the three attempts typically depicted in a heroic quest.

And outside the world of faith, mystery and folklore, the number three also has strong connotations in science and mathematics. It is deeply embedded in the natural world, technology, and human-made systems.

It is a cornerstone in various scientific phenomena and mathematical theories, illustrating an underlying order and symmetry that guides our understanding of the universe.

In physics and chemistry, three classic states of matter describe how particles relate to each other: solid, where particles are closely packed and vibrate in place; liquid, where particles are close together but move more freely; and gas, where particles are far apart and move rapidly.

These three states are observable in everyday life, such as when water freezes into ice (solid), flows as liquid, or boils into steam (gas). The transitions between these states are central to understanding many physical processes.

In biology, the tripartite structure appears in various forms. For example, the fundamental building block of life, the DNA molecule, follows a triple helix model in some organisms.

Also, the human brain is often divided into three main parts: the forebrain, midbrain, and hindbrain, each responsible for different functions and processes.

In mathematics, three is the first odd prime number and the second smallest prime number following two.
It's a number that has fascinated mathematicians for centuries.

The Pythagorean theorem, for example, is based on right-angled triangles, where a fundamental geometric principle relates the three sides.

Euler's famous formula, which connects five of the most important numbers in mathematics, involves using the cube root of unity, another representation of the number three.

Geometry and design often employ the "triangle," a three-sided shape considered one of the most stable and fundamental forms. Architects and engineers utilise this principle to build sturdy structures.

Furthermore, in computer science, the concept of ternary logic, which uses three values instead of the typical two in binary logic, has been explored as an alternative computational approach.

The game theory, often used in economics and social science, also uses three-player games to model complex strategic interactions and these games can reveal insights into how people cooperate, compete, and strategies in various scenarios.

A standard method of understanding data in statistical analysis describes its "three measures of central tendency": the mean, median, and mode.

And when it comes to storytelling and sharing information, the "rule of three" is not just a common trope in storytelling; it is a time-tested principle that seems to tap into fundamental human psychology.

Stories and presentation therefore, that come in threes or with three elements have a satisfying symmetry and rhythm that resonate deeply with readers and listeners.

This pattern is embedded across various genres and cultural contexts, with many examples and interpretations. Many fairy tales, a bedrock of our literary tradition, employ the rule of three to structure their narrative.

Classic stories like the "Three Little Pigs" and "Goldilocks and the Three Bears" are prime examples.

In these tales, the pattern of three offers a clear and memorable sequence: the first situation sets the stage, the second builds tension, and the third resolves the conflict.

The three tasks, characters, or events often allow for a progression of difficulty, complexity, or understanding that helps engage the audience.

But the rule extends far beyond children's stories. In ancient Greek rhetoric, the tripartite structure was used to persuade and argue through ethos, pathos, and logos.

These three modes of persuasion formed the basis for constructing a compelling argument.

The three-act structure has become a foundational technique in modern literature and film.

The first act introduces the characters and conflict, the second develops tension and challenges, and the third brings resolution and closure.

This pattern is evident in countless works, from Shakespearean plays to contemporary Hollywood blockbusters.

Even in speeches and public speaking, using three-part lists or arguments is common. It's no accident that some of the most famous lessons in history have used this structure.

Martin Luther King Jr.'s "I Have a Dream" speech employed the rule of three in various ways, repeating key phrases and structuring thoughts in triads to build rhythm and emphasis.

The power of three also permeates poetry and music.

Whether in the three-line structure of a haiku or the three-chord progression of many popular songs, the number three offers a balance that feels dynamic and stable.

So, all of that is surely enough to convince you that we live in a world governed by the number three, and if not, then let me also share that the rule of three has been examined from psychological perspectives as well.

Cognitive scientists have explored why this pattern is so compelling and found that information presented in threes is more likely to be retained and processed effectively.

Simply put, the brain responds favourably to the structure, making it an assertive communication and presentation tool.

Therefore, when composing that Killer presentation, designing, and delivering slides and information using the power of three is a simple yet irresistible technique you can employ to significant effect.

Thinking back to earlier in this book, creating an agenda and navigation utilising the power of three is a simple yet highly effective means to enhance audience engagement.

And when it comes to the content within, whilst still maintaining the critical mantra of making just one point per slide, using threes to support those points is compelling.

One plays to our deep-seated psychological conditioning to the number three, and one that is also entirely wedded to what has often been termed our reptilian brain.

It involves the basal ganglia, an area of the brain that has been around for a very long time in evolutionary terms, operates subconsciously, governing instincts and deep-seated emotional reactions and decision making,
something which is also sometimes referred to system-a decision making, or as I like to call it our Homer Simpson brain.

Put simply, the world around us then one of three, from three little pigs to three steps on a podium and three wise monkeys we think and feel in threes.

And talking of three wise monkeys, when it comes to the first of those, see no evil, it also points to another critical consideration when creating that killer presentation, what people see, something that I will now enlighten you further on.

#6

Welcome Herr Dumpidump

When it comes to storytelling as an art, a paradoxical or dialectical relationship exists between what we see and hear.

The power of a well-told story lies in just an auditory form, allowing you to conjure up powerful images within your imagination and take you on a personalised magical trip of excitement and delight.

Yet similarly, some argue the power of a visually led tale, such as defined by the cinematic masterpiece, cannot be beaten and that this grip on storytelling is now only tightened in a world increasingly directly delivered through our many screens.

Yet, whilst one may initially seem at odds with the other when combined, they deliver a sensory dimension that unlocks a more extraordinary sensory experience and immersion for the audience.

And this is also entirely true regarding the art of storytelling within presentations, where what we present visually to our audiences can not only provide an enhanced sensory experience, unlocking the angels cocktail explored earlier in this book, but also, critically, the correct visual representation can enhance the ability of the audience to recall the information conveyed at a later date, and in the required level of detail too, which means that to some. Vision is often considered the dominant sense in humans, and a substantial portion of the brain is dedicated to processing visual information.

It is a scientific fact that 30% or more of the cerebral cortex is involved in visual processing, whilst various other parts of the brain are involved in processing different aspects of visual information, such as colour, motion, depth, and shape.

And this relationship between image and brain extends into memory, too.

By better understanding this relationship between images and memory, we can exploit it to enhance the impact of storytelling and presentations.

It starts with encoding and Visualisation:

When we encounter a visual image, the brain processes and encodes the information into a format that can be stored in memory.

Evidence of this is the so-called 'visualisation technique', often used to enhance memory by associating abstract information with images making information more vivid and easier to recall.

This is supported by research showing that people tend to remember images better than words, known as the picture superiority effect.

As to why this is the case, it is thought that images can be encoded both visually and semantically (in terms of meaning).

In contrast, words are typically encoded semantically, so this dual coding of images may make them more memorable.

Additionally, Images that evoke strong emotions or an emotional reaction and aid the release of dopamine, oxytocin, and endorphins, as present in the 'angels-cocktail', also tend to be more easily remembered because of something called 'Emotional Impact', where through activating the 'amygdala', a part of the brain associated with emotions, they further enhance the encoding and storage of memories and information.

And whilst as evidenced above, the relationship between images and memory is multifaceted, involving different cognitive processes, neural mechanisms, and even individual differences in how people process and remember visual information.

The takeout for us is that when it comes to storytelling in presentations, they are a powerful means to drive memory and future recall, along with providing the means to stand out.

As an example of this in action, a few years ago, I was asked to lead a pitch for the programmatic advertising business of a large client for whom we currently needed to hold that assignment.

And anyone who has ever touched the subject of programmatic advertising, in essence, advertising delivered by machines and algorithms, will immediately tell you that this is a complex subject and not one you would typically associate with visual storytelling.

But as hopefully, you will have ascertained by now that I avoid looking at things typically; therefore, visual storytelling was the only way to go.

And this conviction was further enhanced by the fact that we would be competing against several other specialist agencies, all considered more skilled in the art than ourselves.

Not for the first, as anyone who has read my previous writings will attest, I found inspiration in my hobby of origami, the ancient Japanese art of paper folding, in which I have become proficient over the years.

Our story was based on the simple idea that, as in origami, to succeed would need both a narrative and vision married to expertise and process, which must be delivered in the proper order.

And to reinforce this, visually, we utilised an image of a crane that is most recognisable of origami models.

Not only that, but we also created an actual origami, reworked to allow novices to fold easily, that would narrate the presentation and, in the end, leave the audience with their very own crane, a reminder of our production and means to deliver us both standout and critical recall.

And as expected, because it was grounded in storytelling, art and science, our presentation pitch and story stood out, winning the business, and establishing programmatic origami as a real thing.

And when imagery is further extended into a more comprehensive presentation theme, as was the case above, the power of that imagery to drive memory and stand out can be significantly enhanced too.

And using images in presentations can also offer an additional, often unrecognised benefit in our modern, globally delivered world, helping us transcend and translate into language.

For example, if I were to present you with the words 'Herr DumpiDump" and assume that you were not of Norwegian Origins or proficient in its language, then it is unlikely you would have a clue as to who I was referring to.

But I was to present you with it, accompanied by the visual reference to go along with it, of Mr Bump, from the Mr Men cartoon series, your brain can instantly understand that Herr DumpiDump is, in fact, Mr Bump, the character from the 'Mr Men 'series of children's books written by Roger Hargreaves.

Or perhaps, Monsieur Malchance, Herr Beule, Don Chichón, Signor Livido, Meneer Bots, Senhor Pancada or even バンプ氏 (Bumpu-shi), depending on your mother tongue.

So, the power and importance of images in crafting that killer presentation and conveying your story to an audience cannot be ignored nor overstated.

But if images are critical in creating a killer presentation, choosing the right pictures is equally crucial because, put simply, not all images are born equal, as I will now explain.

#7

<u>Try Trump & Trainspotting</u>

It has often been said that a picture can speak a thousand words, and it is a saying that I wholeheartedly agree with.

As we have already explored, the right images bring an essential visual dimension to storytelling and presentations that enhances and helps people decode and critically remember long after being heard.

But note the word 'right' here because it is a simple fact that not all images are equal, and some can even detract and distract from the point they are being used to make.

In my career, I have been fortunate to have worked with some great storytellers and presentation masters, and none more so than a certain David Shing, or Shingy, 'the digital prophet' as he was often known.

And one thing that David and I shared an obsession with was the images that we used in presentations.

As anyone who has seen the 'digital prophet' up close and personal, plying his trade, can attest, many of his images are often unexpected and even shocking, but this is done with absolute intent.

That intent is also the same when it comes to my selections. And that is because images are not born equal when used in a presentation.

While working at AOL with Shingy, as he was generally known, I also dug further into the science of this, and it turns out that science supports this point of view.

Long before chatGPT was even a twinkle in the eye of openAI, and mid journey hadn't even left the station, the principles of AI, although no one called it that at the time) were being applied to the question of what makes an impactful image by a project born from MIT called 'Large-scale Image Memorability', or LaMem, for short, was an online algorithm that aimed to tell you how memorable your photos or images were.

The algorithm, which can still be found at http://memorability.csail.mit.edu/demo.html was claimed by the developers to have a near human consistency of 0.68 and using convolutional neural networks, yes AI before we called it AI, they aimed to show which objects and regions were positively, and negatively, correlated with memorability.

This allowed the creation of memorability maps for each image and provided a concrete method for manipulating image memorability.

LaMem appears to prefer clearly defined subjects.

Images that are popular can often score poorly with LaMem, so you must be the judge of how accurate it is in the real world.

That said, it's still interesting to see how your images score.

As mentioned, it can still be found at the URL above, and for the more technical amongst you, the white paper and API can be found at *http://memorability.csail.mit.edu/index.html* (NB all were still live URLs at the time of writing).

Now, of course, it goes without saying that in its early iteration, at least given this was in 2016 or thereabouts, it did exclude emotion, personal preference, and knowledge of what's photographically interesting, and doubtless, there are large neural datasets now being asked the question using modern AI.

For example, when you ask Google Bard what makes an image memorable, it suggests the following.

"Many factors can contribute to making an image memorable. Some of the most important factors include:

- Uniqueness: A memorable image stands out from the crowd. It may be an unusual or unexpected scene or simply a well-composed and well-executed image.

- Complexity: A complex image requires the viewer to spend some time looking at it to understand it fully and can be achieved with unusual compositions, unexpected juxtapositions, or intricate details.

- Emotion: A memorable image evokes an emotional response in the viewer., be it joy, sadness, anger, or any other emotion. The more powerful the emotional response, the more likely the image will be remembered.

- Storytelling: A memorable image tells a story. This could be a literal story, such as a person's journey, or a more abstract story, such as the story of the human condition and links to the previous points made on complexity and emotion, too.
- Personal connection: A memorable image has a personal connection to the viewer, be it an image of a loved one, a picture of a place that is special to the viewer, or an image that captures a moment in time that the viewer will never forget.

Of course, not all memorable images will have all these qualities.

However, the more of these qualities an image has, the more likely it is to be remembered.

And, of course, AI is often a little loquacious in nature, so it then goes on to add some thoughts or additional tips for taking memorable images which it lists as

- Pay attention to the composition of your images. A well-composed image will be more visually appealing and easier to remember.
- Use strong colours and contrast. This will help to make your images stand out from the crowd.

- Experiment with different angles and perspectives. This can help to create more interesting and dynamic images.

- Be mindful of the light. Good lighting can make a big difference in the quality of your images.

- Take your time. Take your time with the process of taking your images. Take the time to frame your shot carefully and capture the moment in the best possible way.

Now, I don't know about you, but whilst some of this is good advice with which I would concur, a lot of it, especially the latter part, sounds like the sort of waffle you might expect from a junior management consultant, which is all too often what you get from AI at present, so with that in mind, here is an alternative method that I have developed and which you can swear by, quite literally!

This method called the Fearless, fun, and f**k me method, doesn't rely on a complex algorithm or AI but is built on years and years of presentations given and watched, perhaps making it a neural network of the more analogue kind but in so doing it does draw upon the storytelling science we covered earlier in this book.

So then, let's look at how it works.

The first principle, fearless, operates around what I believe is the absolute need to avoid the usual 'safe' stock photographs so beloved of 'PowerPoint designers' within the advertising and marketing agencies within which I work, and which remove all emotion and personality out of presentation through their addition.

Sadly, when it comes to presentations and impactful, memorable images, this kind of unlikely-to-offend or raise-an-eyebrow image is also unlikely to have any impact either, or provoke any memory with the audience afterwards, something which is essential if we are to have a memory benefit from using them.

So, first up, be fearless in your choice of image.

Pick impactful images, make a point, and have that stopping power.

Of course, you need to judge the audience you are presenting to and their risk tolerance, but again, just as with many wrong assumptions in the world of storytelling and presentation writing, assuming anything that is bold or has stopping power might cause offence or be too much is often entirely wrong.

For example. Starting a pitch presentation to a large multinational with a picture of Donald Trump.

Of course not.

Well yes.

To clarify, I am no fan of Donald Trump, the day-glow king of bullshit bingo and certainly no advocate of his policies.

But when it came to starting the pitch presentation to a large multinational corporation that operated within a restricted category, then 'Day-Glo Donald was the perfect choice.

Due to confidentiality, I will not name the client at hand but, like many clients in the modern world, they were wrestling with the challenge of marketing and communicating in a category where a lot of paid media advertising was impossible.

As a critical context, I should also explain what this had to do with the dayglo-Don.

So, a couple of weeks before the pitch presentation, and still wrestling with strategically solving this problem, I found myself at the Cannes Advertising Festival and arriving early for a scheduled meeting with our media partner, Twitter.

Now, as you do at such things, I found myself coffee in hand, engaged in a conversation with Jack Dorsey, who I am sure most of you will know, was the gentleman who founded and ran Twitter long before it became ElonX or whatever it is today.

For someone with such an achievement on his CV, I found Mr Dorsey extraordinarily humble and willing to engage in a conversation rather than hide behind his minions.

For reasons I do not recall, we ended up conversing on the topic of Mr Trump, who at the time was seeking to be elected as president of the US and who at the time most had never considered would be successful in that venture, let alone with the spectre of a repeat performance now looming at the time of writing this book.

Anyway, and perhaps a little provocatively, but hey, that is me, I asked Jack why he continued to allow Trump to use his platform and why on earth he hadn't shut him down.

His answer was short, simple, and as brilliant as you would expect from a gentleman of his stature.

"Digital democracy."

Two simple but compelling words, and elaborating on this statement further, he explained that however distasteful he found Mr Trump and very was a word I recall used if he did not allow him to speak, then he would undermine a fundamental principle of the internet and Twitter at the time, that of digital democracy.

Now, I am 100% certain that today, Mr Dorsey would probably not even recall our conversation, and that was perhaps true the day after, but for me, it stuck in my mind and offered the answer to my pitch conundrum.

Now, the irony of those words, with the benefit of hindsight and history since, is certainly not lost on me.

Still, at the time, it was evident that dear old Donald was already becoming a master of using digital democracy in the form of online platforms, particularly Twitter, to his advantage, something we now know to have also been powered by those lovely folks at Cambridge Analytica and their questionable approach to data collection and privacy.

And thinking about the brief at hand, it was evident that this approach could work for the client, too.

But how do you make that point and make it unforgettable and leap out at them?

Step forward my image of Day-Glo Donald, nothing more, nothing less.

Now, I would venture that using it to make this point, especially when accompanied by the above story, was not as some had feared, an act of stupidity, but rather one of strategic inspiration and one that was made possible by adhering to my first principle of fearless, when choosing images.

And when you show such conviction and bravery, especially when giving presentations, then in my experience, you benefit from unlocking and unleashing some oxytocin in your prospective audience, something that we explored earlier in the science of storytelling part of this book.

The second principle of fun is self-explanatory as it relates to unlocking endorphins within your audience because images, if used correctly, inject subtle and witty humour into the proceedings.

But please note the use of the word subtle and witty here because, as I will touch on, there is no room for the clowns in the world of presentations.

In general, something subtle and witty is defined as clever in a way that is not obvious and subtle humour is generally regarded as not immediately apparent but still makes people smile or laugh, but not out loud.

Ensuring that your images, if aimed at unlocking a subtle dose of endorphins, adhere to this approach also brings with it the additional benefit of delivering a touch of dopamine by making you think or consider it for a moment until the subtle wit it contains becomes evident.

The final part of my image trinity, as it were, is what term the f**k me effect.

As the slightly rude name suggests, a f**k me image makes the user stop, sit up and take notice, even if they have distracted themselves with other things such as a coffee or their mobile device, the curse of the modern presentation, sadly.

When I was working with Shingy, we sometimes referred to them as the Twitter slide, which people instantly wanted to take a picture of and then tweet.

And when that happened, you instantly knew that your point had not just been made but also remembered and shared – the holy grail of presentation reaction.

Generally, such a slide would, as well as a highly impactful and memorable image, also contain some simple sharp copy, much like that brilliant billboard or magazine ad, to help it burn itself into your audience's memory.

To provide some examples, one slide I was fond of using when talking to the world of digital and data to find audiences was a highly memorable image of the cookie monster wearing sunglasses accompanied by the copy line of "people are people, not cookies."

Similarly, when discussing the need for more data experts, not just databases, I would use a picture of an origami Yoda (folded by myself in case you were wondering) with the headline FROM data death stars TO data Jedi's.

And sometimes, the perfect F**K me image falls into your lap.

The best example I can offer is an image I use when speaking to the importance of online reviews in trust-building and purchase decisions in the modern world.

The image in question mimics the infamous poster for the movie Trainspotting, and on it, someone has placed a fake one-star Amazon rating with a review that states, "There are no trains in this movie at all.

Brilliant, although to my memory of the actual movie, perhaps flawed as there was a brief train appearance at one point.

But regardless, this is an example of an image that does all three, be fearless, fun and deliver f**k me, and in so doing, also provides a massive dose of the storytelling chemicals we discussed earlier in this book.

And yes, before you ask, I do get the irony of using a trainspotting-related image to deliver chemical alteration to an audience, as a client I was training once pointed out to me.

And just a word of caution, especially with the f**k me images, is to ensure you use them sparingly, and indeed, I would not suggest ever using one right after another.

Say, for example, your presentation is fifty slides long.

Four or five such images max, and think about where they are placed, and use them to either help reengage your audience where they may have tuned out or introduce a new section or area of story focus.

Before we move on to the fascinating world of fonts and colour, there are two or three other important things to highlight regarding the presentation image and its use.

Firstly, finding good images is not hard, but it does take some time and practice.

Whenever I see or find an interesting image, even if I do not have an immediate role for it in mind, I grab it and keep it.

Doing so has enabled me to build, over a few years, a fantastic collection of images that I can quickly dip into for impact and often my inspiration.

Secondly, the rapid rise of AI tools that allow you to create high-quality images from a few carefully chosen words or rework an existing one into a better context means that the excuse of I am not creative or don't know where to find them is not an excuse that should wash.

For example, the website www.photofunia.com allows you to create engaging images for free, with a few clicks and no more.

And whilst a little more complex, midjourney.io represents the new breed of image generation tools that should at least be tried by those aiming to create a visually impactful presentation deck.

And when you are entirely comfortable that your static image game is strong, why not introduce a little movement but add some subtle video backgrounds to your slides?

Again, this is not rocket-science, and PowerPoint itself now includes a library of such content to use, whilst alongside the AI image generation tools, there are also similar ones focused on creating videos and a quick Google search of AI platforms to help make videos will offer you a selection of both free and paid options.

A non-AI alternative to this is also to arm yourself with YouTube and something called 4k video downloader, a freemium plugin available via a simple Google or DuckDuckGo search.

And thirdly and finally, I must add a few words on using GIFs as images.

GIFs, which stands for Graphics Interchange Format, are a popular bitmap image format introduced by CompuServe as long ago as 1987 when the internet was still just a twinkle in the eye of Tim Burners Lee.

GIFs are a widely recognized and used image format, primarily known for their ability to display short, looping animations, something that can make them a valuable tool in presentations, too.

However, despite this, using GIFs for this purpose can badly backfire due to the following.

Firstly, most gifs, by their nature, are low-resolution. Therefore, when added to a slide and expanded into a larger screen, they can look highly pixelated, unclear, and often just downright awful.

Secondly, the things that make them GIFs can also become the thing that makes them annoying, their looping.

So carefully consider how long the image will be shown, and if it means that the looping will be seen five, six or even more times, then it is best avoided.

In addition, if the loop is very overt, i.e. obvious, avoid it.

Conversely, good gifs are often ones with just a subtle touch of movement in them, a shimmer, a slight touch of movement and where the looping is almost if not entirely invisible.

Also, avoid putting more than one on a single slide. I have seen some dreadful PowerPoint crimes where three or four GIFs are placed on the same slide. In short, don't and that goes for using GIFs that are MEMEs, too.

In the digital age, "meme" refers to content that spreads virally online, often in images, videos, and text. These internet memes can evolve and spread rapidly, sometimes reaching worldwide popularity within days.

Internet memes can be humorous, satirical, political, or based on many other themes, but let me assure you, they have no place whatsoever in a good presentation. None whatsoever.

So now we have addressed the not-insignificant topic of image use in presentations; let us move on to one which, for me, has equal importance but is often overlooked and ignored, and that is why you should give a FONT about fonts and colours.

#8

Give a font about the fonts & colours.

Most people reading this book will have heard of the American Tex-Mex restaurant chain Taco Bell.

Founded by Glen Bell in 1962 in Downey, California, the brand has since become one of the leading chains in the fast-food industry.

But how many of you will have heard of their one-time competitor, Fast Taco?

Very few of you, if any, I would venture, and that is because when it came to font choices,

Taco Bell chose wisely, whilst Fast Taco did not, choosing a font which made the word FAST look more like the word FART.

The rest, as they say, is history because who, being honest, wants to be reminded of one of the side effects of eating Tacos after all?

Okay, this story may be partially accurate in a historical sense, but regardless, it speaks to the importance of Fonts and choosing the right ones when constructing your presentation.

Consider a simple phrase like "I will never forget you." If we write it using a smooth, friendly font, it comes across as caring, warm, and full of positive emotions.

Yet, write the same thing in a jagged, edgy font, and it evokes the sensation of a good horror movie, where the person writing it will not stop until they have tracked you down, and nothing, it seems, can stop them!

As another example, earlier in this book, I referenced a presentation I once created about the world of digital media streaming, which borrowed its inspiration from Star Wars, entitled The Streaming Wars.

In constructing this presentation, I used a licensed Star Wars font called Star Jedi to visually convey the inspiration and story.

Had I chosen not to do this and instead gone with the choice of comic-sans, I will guarantee you that, even with the right images, my presentation would not have delivered the impact or effect I intended, and the same would have been true had I chosen the most vanilla of fonts, Arial.

Now, whilst there may be nothing wrong with these fonts in many people's minds, in the world of exciting presentations, Arial is the perfect way to say you don't care, whilst there is absolutely nothing funny about Comic Sans. Nothing at all.

And don't, at this stage, allow yourself to fall foul of the font police, either.

'That's not our official font' or 'they won't have that installed on their machines' are the standard mating calls of such individuals.

Yes, of course, that may be true on both counts, but the upside of the effort this requires is significantly more than the downside of bowing to the font police, in my experience.

Now, at this stage, to illustrate the importance of fonts and show you how, just as with images, they are heavily related to our reptilian brains and against which 95% of our decision-making is still related, along with how we recognise and remember, let's indulge ourselves in a little quiz.

Below are five snippets of fonts used in well-known logos that do not show the whole word and font.

But can you still identify the brands from the small piece that remains?

Unless you have been stranded on a Pacific Island for fifty years or so, of course you can.

Star Wars, Cadbury's, Disney, LinkedIn & Nintendo, even with only a tiny portion on show, the power of fonts makes the brands instantly recognisable and does so through the power of memory.

So, when it comes to creating that killer presentation, it does pay to give a font about the fonts you use, and the same is true for the colours you choose, too.

Earlier in this book, we explored how, as visually driven creatures, what we see is often critical to our decision-making and memory.

A big part of this is also related to the use of colour.

For most people, colour is always around us, but as such, we take it for granted and forget its importance in impacting our decision-making and emotional chemistry.

Yet, take it away, and then suddenly, its importance in our everyday world is evident for all to see.

Imagine, if you will, a can of Coca-Cola, but not in its traditional red, but just in black and white and nothing else.

Alternatively, imagine a colourful bowl of M&M's, the small, round, candy-coated chocolates introduced in 1941 and have since become one of the world's most popular and recognisable sweets.

Now imagine that bowl without the colour again, just a bowl of white-looking pills, which doesn't look alluring.

Or imagine ordering your Big Mac and fries, only for them to be given to you, not in the usual red box, but in a plain white box with black writing and nothing else.

And imagine going into Google to find that the brightly coloured logo is now just black letters on white.

Not only is colour integral to how we see, process, and remember the world around us, but it is also a critical element in eliciting emotional responses, something we have already explored in this book.

Red is often associated with passion, love, danger, and energy. In some cultures, red represents luck and prosperity.

Blue symbolises calmness, stability, trust, and tranquillity. In many corporate settings, blue is used to convey reliability.

Green represents nature, growth, harmony, and fertility. In Western cultures, it can also symbolise money.

Yellow is often associated with happiness, sunshine, warmth, and optimism. In some contexts, it can also indicate caution.

Purple has long been associated with royalty and luxury due to the rarity and expense of purple dye. It can also represent creativity and mystery.

Black denotes power, elegance, and formality. In many cultures, it's linked with death and mourning.

White represents purity, innocence, and simplicity. In some Eastern cultures, white is associated with death and mourning.

Orange combines the energy of red and the happiness of yellow. It is associated with enthusiasm, joy, and the tropics.

Brown evokes feelings of stability, reliability, and earthiness. It's often used to represent things that are natural or organic.

Gray can be seen as a neutral colour, conveying formality, professionalism, and sophistication. It can also be associated with dullness or a lack of emotion.

Pink has historically been associated with femininity, romance, and softness. It can also represent hope and compassion.

Gold symbolises wealth, grandeur, and prosperity. It's also linked with achievement and high quality.

And silver represents sleekness, high tech, and modernity. It can also symbolise wealth, as gold does, but more understatedly.

Now, in the past, when I have spoken on this topic, I have been asked about the issue of colour blindness.

Colour blindness, also known as colour vision deficiency (CVD), is a condition in which an individual's perception of colours differs from that of a normal human eye.

This can be due to an absence or malfunction of one or more types of colour receptors (cone cells) in the eye.

The most common form of colour blindness is Red-Green colour blindness, and other types of colour blindness include Protanopia, which is the inability to perceive red light, and Deuteranopia, which is the inability to perceive green light. There is also protanomaly, which has a reduced sensitivity to red light, and deuteranomaly, which has a reduced sensitivity to green light.

Another form of colour blindness is blue-yellow colour blindness.

There are two main types: Tritanopia, which is the inability to perceive blue light, and Tritanomaly, which is reduced sensitivity to blue light.

Total colour blindness, where the person can only see in shades of grey and is known as Achromatopsia, is very rare, affecting only about 1 in 30,000 to 50,000 people.

Interestingly, colour blindness is primarily a genetic condition where men are much more likely to be colour-blind than women, as the genes responsible for the most common forms of colour blindness are on the X chromosome.

It's estimated that approximately 8-10% of the male population and under 1% of the female population have some form of colour vision deficiency, most of which are cases of red-green colour blindness.

So, what this means when it comes to presentations is simple.

Firstly, avoid mixing red and green colours on a single slide.

Similarly, avoid mixing blue and yellow together on slides, too.

And that leaves just one question for me: who will tell Microsoft and Google about this critical headline?

And talking of headlines, when it comes to creating that killer presentation, the headlines or lack of them, can make all the difference, something we will now explore in more depth.

#9

Submarine hides in the sea.

It is undeniable that through their design, PowerPoint, and Keynote (if you have the Mac inclination) have created an unspoken rule that any presentation slide containing text or information must also have a headline.

But here is the thing: you may not need one at all.

'Federal agents raid gun shop and finds weapons.'

'World Bank says poor need more money.'

'China may be using the sea to hide its submarines.'

These are all actual headlines from real-world news articles that add zero to the proceeding and merely state the obvious, and the same is entirely true with a lot of presentation headlines, too.

So, the first thing to consider is whether you need a headline at all, and by a headline, I mean that line of text that sits at the top of your slide in the top left-hand corner. As an avid student of simplicity,

I am a huge fan of dropping headlines and instead just using a single statement headline in the middle of a slide.

Not only does this support the earlier rules I set out about making just one point per page, but it also draws the audience's attention and gives them no doubt about what to focus on.

It can exist as a single line of copy or be paired with a powerful image to aid memory, as we covered earlier, but either way, the net effect will be to grab your audience's attention.

But regardless of which, it should adhere to two simple rules.

Firstly, make it as short as it can be.

Secondly, make it exciting and memorable, too.

These are essential because your headline is designed to serve one clear purpose.

That is, sit at the top of your slide and introduce the content or data below, exciting an audience to learn more.

Given this, any headline must be much less than any content it introduces and, as such, ideally never extend beyond a single line in length.

While this may sound like common sense and an easy thing to achieve,

Yet, I consistently see slide headlines that could pass as entire presentations, seeking to summarise and share the contents below within the headline and serving not to convince but merely confuse an audience.

From a personal perspective, if my headline extends beyond one line, then I take that as an indicator that it is too long, too loquacious, and as a result, set myself the task of rewriting it again to make it shorter and, generally, by implication, sharper.

Admittedly, good headline writing is a real art and, like most arts, requires practice.

Yet you don't have to look too far to find real inspiration and insight into how you can do this.

For many years, newspapers have refined and perfected the art of sharp and witty headline writing, and none so more than what is often termed the tabloid press.

Whilst some of their content may be questionable and certainly not to everyone's taste, it is undeniable that when it comes to headline writing, those folks are absolute masters.

From the infamous UK Sun newspaper headline,
'Freddie Starr ate my hamster',

to a more recent headline, '
I'm with stupid',

which accompanied a picture of US politicians Sarah Palin and Donald Trump together, some of their creations are absolute masterpieces of copywriting.

And in case you still need to work it out, sharp and exciting headlines are also a fantastic means to add further small doses of the Angels Cocktail to an audience, slide by slide.

But headlines, or not, the one thing that truly, separates a good presentation from a truly dreadful one is the point at which presentation and presenter collide where the biggest single mistake is often made, and where one plus one equals zero – something we will now examine in more detail.

#10

<u>One plus one equals zero.</u>

A presentation comprises two parts: the presentation or story and the presenter or storyteller who delivers it.

However, whilst the two parts will ideally work together seamlessly to deliver a compelling presentation or story, they should never be a carbon copy of each other.

Instead, the headline act should always be the presenter or storyteller with the story or presentation a well-crafted support to aid them in delivery.

Yet time and time again, I sit through presentations where this is precisely how they are delivered, and the presenter reads out each slide and each word contained within each slide as if driven by some unwritten rule that this must be so.

Yet the reality of doing this is just the creation of white noise.

That is because reading out every single word on a slide religiously, in effect, cancels out that slide, as the audience struggles to work out if they are listening to you, the presenter or storyteller, or should just be reading the story put up in front of them.

And worse still, some presenters, most likely driven by nerves or a lack of comfort with their content, suddenly become highly loquacious, speaking many long words but not saying anything of real meaning or value to play back the meaning of that word.

This means that a slide, which should be thirty seconds or less, becomes one that takes minutes and loses both the attention and goodwill of your audience.

Another consequence is that when people become loquacious in their delivery of content, they also tend to increase the speed at which they speak, making it even harder to follow their words, not to mention impacting their ability to breathe and inhale enough oxygen to continue with the task.

My advice is to address this and avoid the creation of presentation white noise by doing two things.

Firstly, try to work to at most thirty seconds per slide.

Now, of course, that is not a hard or fast rule.

But if you follow the earlier rule about one point per slide, then it is unlikely that you will need to spend more than that on most slides and in so doing, you will avoid the risk of coming across as rambling and trying to over-explain or present your points.

Secondly, and even more simply, take a pause.

If you watch excellent presenters and storytellers go about their art, not only are they not loquacious in their delivery, but they also are masters of the dramatic pause as a powerful means of injecting further anticipation or expectation into an audience.

And those pauses can be either between slides, during them, or even both.

The critical point is that silence can be golden when it comes to storytelling, and at the very least, silence is undoubtedly better than bullshit, as they say.

Of course, pausing for too long can derail this and make people believe that you are either beset by nerves or have forgotten the story you are telling, but pausing for one or two seconds between points or four or five seconds between slides will never, in my experience deliver this result, but will not only bring confidence and calmness to your storytelling but also allow you time to partake of some essential oxygen too - very handy for dealing with nerves when presenting.

And as far as our tenth principle or tip goes, that is it. In short, you are the storyteller there to tell the story, not just read it, and if you apply that rule, then your story and storytelling will work hand in hand and not equate to one plus one equals zero.

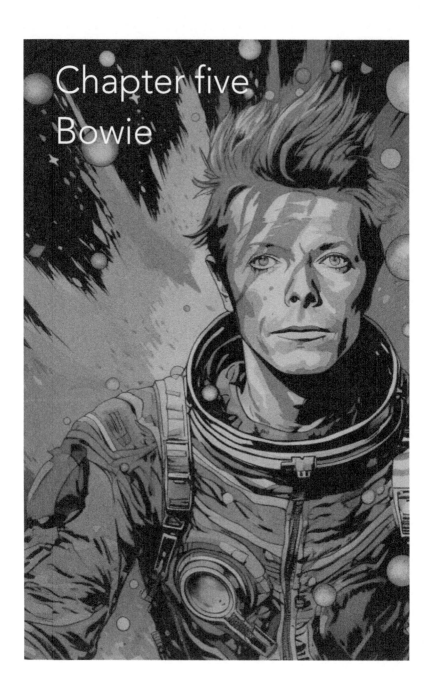

Chapter five
Bowie

I don't know where I'm going from here but I promise it won't be boring.

David Bowie - songwriter.

Let's finish this book by talking about David Bowie.

Not only was he a powerful storyteller, as evidenced earlier in this book when we looked at his use of the story spine, but he also possessed another unique attribute that makes that storytelling even more powerful.

And that unique attribute was his inherent ability to reinvent himself and the theatre with which he told and performed those stories.

From Major Tom to Ziggy Stardust and his final work, Dark Star, he was constantly able to reinvent how he showed up and told or performed those stories, bringing a further dimension.

And when we apply that perspective to business presentations, doing something similar is often a way to stand out from the crowd.

And that is because, when it comes to the world of presentations and presentation giving, there is a simple, if often unspoken, truth that genuinely creative and innovative presenters have already known, and that is simply that sometimes the best PowerPoint is no PowerPoint.

We have become so dependent on PowerPoint or Keynote in the modern business world that the mere thought of a presentation without using either seems like no presentation.

In fact, for many, the mere act of even conceiving to give a presentation without either of these aids would instantly equate to a failure to do their job, a reason for them to be relieved of their duties due to a dereliction of theirs.
Yet when you challenge yourself and, in so doing, your intended audience to a presentation without PowerPoint, you

are opening almost limitless possibilities and means to enhance your storytelling and, in so doing, deliver a story that cannot be forgotten.

Think about it: when was the last time you saw a politician give a PowerPoint presentation?

Okay, so maybe in today's world, that is not a good example, but putting the current lack of political competency aside, I bet that at some time in your career, you have encountered a presentation which was delivered without it, and I would venture too that it is one you will still now remember or that stick in your mind above all those other PowerPoint laden encounters.

Don't get me wrong; I am not advocating that you delete PowerPoint or Keynote from your systems, God forbid.

Nor am I suggesting that when appropriately used, as I have shown you, it can be done earlier in this book; it cannot deliver fantastic impact and stand out, too, and is a genuinely powerful business communication tool.

No, I am merely suggesting that the next time you are tasked with telling a story through a presentation, you stop for a few seconds and think about how you might do it for once without using PowerPoint or keynote slides.

Now, of course, the answer may quickly reveal itself to be PowerPoint or Keynote based, but it also may not, and that few seconds thinking, what if could revolutionise your storytelling journey, not to mention your reputation as a storyteller too?
For those who have already undertaken such an approach, the ability to do this will be entirely evident and something they understand to be possible.

Indeed, I currently enjoy the pleasure of working with Amazon, which, as many will know, operates a no PowerPoint in meetings policy, and whilst that brings other challenges, it ensures that real thought and purpose are required in creating a stimulus for meetings and telling a compelling story to start.

However, for those who have yet to consider a world beyond PowerPoint presentations, doing so might seem like a utopian dream or ambition with no evident starting point then.

So, with that in mind, I am going to conclude this book with some examples of where I have done this previously and told stories or given presentations with no PowerPoint or Keynote in sight but rather with other storytelling aids, from Instagram to origami and Lego, are firmly in the frame.

The first example relates to a client I mentioned earlier regarding using the story of Kintsugi. In this instance, it relates to how we delivered the final pitch presentation following that initial storytelling.

The client in question, whom I will not name for obvious reasons, presented us with a strategic brief for launching a new EV or electric vehicle.

At the time, they had no heritage in this space and were entering a marketplace where Tesla was the dominant force and, in effect, the watchword for electric cars.
What they did have, however, was a patent for the use of the word digital and a proven heritage in using this both in design and marketing to significant effect.

They also had a well-known reputation for not paying attention to PowerPoint presentations and lacking tolerance for indulging their agency partners in giving them.

The net effect of this was that, very quickly, they would turn to their laptops or mobiles and switch their attention elsewhere.

So, what to do?

Well, two things.

We decided to write our strategic presentation as a simple graphical book, one that they could take away with them at the end and which would reprise our strategic story, a story that we would first tell through an experience.

Using two different rooms, we composed an exhibition of two halves.

The first half told the story of the old, electric car and how, from the Sinclair C5, one of which we hired to park in the room, to a Wall of Elon, it was a fight they likely would not win.

The second room then told the story of the new, the digital, setting up the premise that, were they to launch the world's first digital car, they were indeed a place they could win. And it worked.

For twenty minutes or so, we held their attention, selling our brave strategy through even braver storytelling.

And I remember a comment from a colleague afterwards that made me smile.

Commenting on the presentation, he remarked,
"I have no idea how you conceived or created that as you did, but my god, did that work incredibly well."

My next two examples and note that none of these are in chronological order, relate to the world of technology and data.

In the world of data and technology, especially in the world of the agency, there is a belief that storytelling is blasphemy and that making it simple and stepping outside of PowerPoint is somehow doing a disservice to its complexity and importance.

In my eyes, that is nonsense, confusing, and not convincing; an audience never works, and I would venture the core reason many ad tech companies never succeed or sell their wares.

With that in mind, I wanted to make only one critical point when asked to present to an internal think tank about our future approach to data and technology.

And that was this.

Rather than continue previous attempts to create a giant database or data tool that could solve all problems, a data death star, as I called it.

Instead, we should focus on hiring more experts and empowering more people with data skills and understanding, finding the data Jedi, as I call it.

So, how do we get this simple but critical idea across? Simple, create some origami.

Drawing on my skills and side line in crafting origami, I created an individual origami Yoda for each meeting attendees in the colours of their agency as a further touch.

Then, come the day of the meeting, when everyone else focused on adding to the confusion with the use of complex PowerPoint presentations laden with what I call the wiring diagrams, complex box and line diagrams that make sense only to the author but never to the audience; I merely removed the lid from the box in which I transported the origami, handed them out and then told a short 2-3 minute story about why we needed more data Jedi and not another data death star.

The presentation was done, and the point was made and delivered without a single PowerPoint slide shown!

Similarly, when I wanted to make the point at the start of a workshop session on data that failure would likely be the outcome without a vision or story to guide things, I turned to using Lego to deliver the story.

To tell that story, I gave everyone a small Lego set, but without any pictures or instructions included.

Instead, it was supplied in a plain white box, telling the story through the experience of trying to build the model without any guide or instructions, which, as you would expect, no one could achieve.

Again, the story was delivered, and the point was made. And when asked to deliver a presentation to our partners on Instagram, what would be the best medium to do so?

Instagram, of course.

No really!

Instagram is a fantastic platform to create and deliver a presentation, not least because it is billed as a storytelling platform by its owners, Meta.

And whilst it might sound complex, only three alterations are needed.

Firstly, images must be square to fit the Instagram window, with text in the comments.

Secondly, the presentation needs to be written or loaded backwards.

Finally, when the time comes to give the presentation, you need to mirror your phone to the presentation screen, but there are many apps to do so, not least Apple Airplay itself if you are using an iPhone.

It also adds another benefit: to see the presentation afterwards, people only need to go to Instagram and follow, avoiding the usual Can you send a PDF or PPTX file challenges.

And if it still sounds a bit odd, visit Instagram and *@goldgreedandgood* to see how I used this technique for a presentation on cryptocurrency.

While the above examples are all ones which actively seek to avoid PowerPoint or Keynote use, another trick is to combine little moments of theatre or surprise and delight using non-PowerPoint media or formats.

For example, when once presenting to a client about voice and the use of Alexa skills whilst using a main presentation delivered in PowerPoint, we asked Alexa herself to tell the short story of how we did this, providing an unexpected and exciting break in the slides and one which also showed we also could practice what we preached too!

But now, I need to add a word of caution.

While such theatre can be compelling and impactful, enhancing a presentation and story to significant effect, there is a line that should always be drawn.

And that is, it should be relevant and there to enhance, not the main event itself.

As an example of this in action, I led a pitch for a gaming client many years ago, which we won with a little bit of theatrical enhancement.

By creating our presentation as an interactive deck of cards, using Adobe Flash at the time, we could add a little fun and theatre that the client loved.

However, getting to the main point of the story, on the day of the pitch, the clients arrived two hours early for our meeting.
When asked why, we were informed that the agency before us had all walked into the pitch room dressed as Jockeys, at which point, they all got up and left in haste, proving that while clever pitch theatre can be a good thing, no one ever loves a clown.

And finally, sometimes the best thing to present with is absolutely nothing at all.

If pressed on who I regard to be the most extraordinary presenter I have ever witnessed, I would not hesitate to respond with David Bell.

A one-time CEO of IPG and advisor to Tim Armstrong during my time at AOL, David could hold a room and tell a story with nothing more than a scrap of paper held in his hand.

He is a true master of storytelling and worked with only his sharp wit and mind.

So then that is it.

The end of this story, but hopefully just the beginning of yours, and one where you will now unleash Bond's storytelling power, delivered with Bowie's flair.

Thank you for reading and I will end of what is perhaps one of the most well-known business storytelling quotes of all time...

The most powerful person in the world is the storyteller.

Steve Jobs

Printed in Great Britain
by Amazon